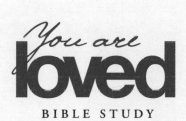

BIBLE STUDY

Sally Clarkson & Angela Perritt

You are loved

BIBLE STUDY

Embracing
God's Love *for* You

women of faith

TYNDALE
MOMENTUM

An Imprint of
Tyndale House Publishers, Inc.

Visit Women of Faith at www.womenoffaith.com.

Visit Tyndale online at www.tyndale.com.

Visit Tyndale Momentum online at www.tyndalemomentum.com.

TYNDALE, Tyndale's quill logo, *Tyndale Momentum*, and the Tyndale Momentum logo are registered trademarks of Tyndale House Publishers, Inc. Tyndale Momentum is an imprint of Tyndale House Publishers, Inc., Carol Stream, Illinois. *Women of Faith* is a trademark of Women of Faith LLC.

You Are Loved Bible Study: Embracing God's Love for You

Previously published in 2014 as *You Are Loved: Embracing the Everlasting Love God Has for You* by Love God Greatly under ISBN 978-1-4993-2875-2. First printing by Tyndale House Publishers, Inc., in 2015.

Designed by Stephen Vosloo

Unless otherwise indicated, all Scripture quotations are taken from the New American Standard Bible,® copyright © 1960, 1962, 1963, 1968, 1971, 1972, 1973, 1975, 1977, 1995 by The Lockman Foundation. Used by permission.

Scripture quotations marked NIV are taken from the Holy Bible, *New International Version,® NIV.®* Copyright © 1973, 1978, 1984, 2011 by Biblica, Inc.® (Some quotations may be from the earlier NIV edition, copyright © 1984.) Used by permission. All rights reserved worldwide.

Printed in the United States of America

21   20   19   18   17   16
7   6   5   4   3

Sally

May all who read this book find the always-abiding, never-changing, generous-beyond-our-imagination love of God. May He bless you to the bottom of your toes and fill every fiber of your being with a smile because of your preciousness to Him.

Angela

This book is dedicated to my Lord and Savior, Jesus Christ; my wonderfully supportive husband and family; and my dearly loved friends who do not know God's love for them yet. This book is written from my heart to yours, and all for God's glory. My prayer is that you will know the extent of God's love for you after reading this book.

Contents

Foreword

"I HAVE LOVED YOU with an everlasting love" (Jeremiah 31:3). . . .
When the God of the universe spoke those words to *all* of humanity,
it changed everything. And those simple but profound words can
change everything for you, me, and everyone in the world.

If you've known those words since you were a child, perhaps
you take them lightly and are hesitant to embrace them for yourself. If you have no concept of the love of God, you might wonder
what in the world these words could mean for you personally.

Wherever you are in your understanding of God's love for you,
the little book you hold in your hand will help . . . and encourage you to embrace the love of God . . . not just for yourself and
your family but maybe even in a far broader sense. It will help
you understand His love for each and every person in the world.
What kind of love is that!

Whether you enjoy the study in those quiet moments when
you're alone or in a small group of friends, our prayer is that you
will embrace the reality of His profound love for you. Perhaps
you'll even find yourself humming an old tune you heard as a
child, "Jesus loves me. This I know. For the Bible tells me so." His
love changes everything. Even you and me.

Mary Graham

Introduction

AS THE TWO OF US gathered in Colorado last summer, we dreamed of writing a book together that would inspire, encourage, and point women to the Lord. After prayer and lots of talking, we decided that if a woman truly understands how deeply she is loved, she is free to grow into the potential loveliness that God created her to have. When a woman feels truly loved, she is confident in herself, she is more generous of heart, and her faith grows strong because of the deep acceptance she receives and lives in from her Creator.

Our Bible study has grown out of our own understanding of God's abiding love. It is our hope and prayer that as you grasp this important spiritual foundation, you will be transformed forever. May God's love flow through your life.

Sally and Angela

How to S.O.A.P.

WE'RE PROUD OF YOU.

We really are . . . we want *you* to know that.

We're proud of you for making the commitment to be in God's Word . . . to read it each day and apply it to *your* life . . . the beautiful life our Lord has given *you*.

Before we get started, we want to explain what the S.O.A.P. method is and why you should use it during your quiet time.

Why S.O.A.P. It?

It's one thing to simply read Scripture, but when you interact with it, when you learn to slow down to *really* read a passage, suddenly words start popping off the page. By applying S.O.A.P. to the verses you read, you will be able to dig deeper into Scripture and "see" more than if you simply read the verses and then go on your merry way. We encourage you to use the S.O.A.P. Journal pages found at the end of each week's reading. Take time each day to read the passage, and then S.O.A.P. the designated verses. We think you'll be amazed as you see for yourself how much more you get out of your daily reading.

What Does S.O.A.P. Mean?

S: The *S* stands for Scripture. As you write out the passage, you'll be amazed at what God will reveal to you just because you took the time to slow down and write out what you are reading!

O: The *O* stands for Observation. What do you see in the verses that you're reading? Who is the audience? Is there a repetition of words? What words stand out to you?

A: The *A* stands for Application. God's Word becomes personal when you discover how to apply it for yourself. What is God saying to you today? How can you apply what you just read to your own personal life? What changes do you need to make? Is there an action that you need to take?

P: And finally, *P* stands for Prayer. Pray God's Word back to Him. If He has revealed something to you during this time in His Word, pray about it. Confess any sin He has revealed in your life.

Studying God's Word like this can take as little or as long as you have time to give. Some days it can take just ten or fifteen minutes; other days, longer.

How Do I S.O.A.P.?

Here is an example based on Colossians 1:5-8. (We've included a few additional comments in italics.)

S: "The faith and love that spring from the hope that is stored up for you in heaven and that you have already heard about in the word of truth, the gospel that has come to you. All over the world this gospel is bearing fruit and growing, just as it has been doing among you since the day you heard it and understood God's grace in all its truth. You learned it from Epaphras, our dear fellow servant, who is a faithful minister of Christ on our behalf, and who also told us of your love in the Spirit." (Colossians 1:5-8, NIV)

O: *You might just bullet your observations . . . what you're seeing at first glance when looking at the verses.*

- When you combine faith and love, you get hope.
- We have to remember that our hope is in heaven . . . it is yet to come.
- The gospel is the word of truth.
- The gospel is continually bearing fruit and growing from the first day to the last.
- It just takes one person to change a whole community . . . Epaphras.

A: Something that stood out to me today was how God used one man, Epaphras, to change a whole town! I was reminded that we are simply called to tell others about Christ . . . it's God's job to spread the gospel . . . to grow it and have it bear fruit. Verse 6 says, "All over the world this gospel is bearing fruit and growing, just as it has been doing among you since the day you heard it and understood God's grace in all its truth."(NIV)

Isn't it fun when God's Word becomes so alive and speaks directly where you are? Our prayer today is that you and all the women involved in this Bible study will understand God's grace and have a thirst for His Word.

I (Angela) wrote this quote from my Bible commentary in my study guide: "God's Word is not just for our information; it for our transformation."[1]

P: Dear Lord, please help me to be an "Epaphras" . . . to tell others about You and then leave the results in Your loving hands. Please

---

[1] *Life Application Study Bible*, New International Version (Carol Stream, IL: Tyndale, 2005), 2002.

help me to understand and apply what I have read today to my life personally, thereby becoming more and more like You each and every day. Help me to live a life that bears the "fruit" of faith and love . . . anchoring my hope in heaven, not here on earth. Help me to remember that the *best* is yet to come!

We hope this explanation helps you today as you learn to dig deeper into God's Word.

And remember; just take it one day at a time. Write your thoughts as you respond to what God has shown you through His Word.

The most important ingredients in the S.O.A.P. method are *your* interaction with God's Word and your *application* of His Word to *your* life as the Spirit speaks to your heart.

The point is to fully meditate and take in each and every word in the passage for the day.

Psalm 1:1-3 says:

Blessed is the man . . . [whose] delight is in the law of the LORD,
And in His law he meditates day and night.
He will be like a tree firmly planted by streams of water,
Which yields its fruit in its season
And its leaf does not wither;
And in whatever he does, he prospers.

True meditation involves taking time to chew on the passage before moving on. As the seventeenth-century English clergyman Thomas Brooks wrote in his classic book, *Precious Remedies against Satan's Devices*: "Remember, it is not hasty reading but serious meditating upon holy and heavenly truths, that make them prove sweet and profitable to the soul. It is not the bee's touching of the flower [that] gathers honey but her abiding for a time upon the flower, which draws out the sweet. It is not he who reads most but he who meditates most, who will prove the choicest, sweetest, wisest and strongest Christian."

It's one thing to talk about how much God loves you, but it's something entirely different to open God's Word and read for yourself how dearly loved you are. Sally and I intentionally developed the reading plan you'll find on the next two pages with you in mind. Sure, we add in stories that showcase how God has personally revealed His love to us, but we don't want you to stop once you've read our accounts. We want you to take your own journey through Scripture. We want you to read for yourself how loved you are. It's one thing to be told that God loves you, but when you read His words for yourself, that truth becomes personal and believable. Join us as we dig into God's Word, day by day, verse by verse, for the next eight weeks, and see for yourself how much you are loved!

S.O.A.P READING PLAN

Read the full passage for each day, and then apply the S.O.A.P. method to the designated verses.

S—Scripture • O—Observation • A—Application • P—Prayer

	READ	S.O.A.P.
WEEK 1	**HE CALLS US BELOVED**	
Monday	Psalm 139	Psalm 139:7-10
Tuesday	Romans 8:35-39	Romans 8:37-39
Wednesday	Zephaniah 3:17	Zephaniah 3:17
Thursday	Isaiah 43:1-7	Isaiah 43:1, 4
Friday	Psalm 86:15	Psalm 86:15

	READ	S.O.A.P.
WEEK 2	**KNOWING GOD**	
Monday	Ephesians 1:17-19	Ephesians 1:17-19
Tuesday	Colossians 1:9-14	Colossians 1:9-10
Wednesday	Jeremiah 24:6-7	Jeremiah 24:7
Thursday	1 John 5:20	1 John 5:20
Friday	Jeremiah 31:33-34	Jeremiah 31:33-34

	READ	S.O.A.P.
WEEK 3	**THE RIVAL**	
Monday	1 Peter 5:6-9	1 Peter 5:8
Tuesday	Revelation 12:10-12	Revelation 12:10
Wednesday	Romans 8:1-4	Romans 8:1
Thursday	1 Peter 2:9	1 Peter 2:9
Friday	Lamentations 3:22-23	Lamentations 3:22-23

	READ	S.O.A.P.
WEEK 4	**GOD LOVES YOU**	
Monday	Romans 5:6-11	Romans 5:6, 8
Tuesday	Ephesians 2:1-5	Ephesians 2:4
Wednesday	Ephesians 2:6-10	Ephesians 2:8-9
Thursday	1 John 4:10-12	1 John 4:10-12
Friday	Hebrews 4:15-16	Hebrews 4:15-16

	READ	S.O.A.P.
WEEK 5	**YOU CAN TRUST HIM**	
Monday	Psalm 84	Psalm 84:11-12
Tuesday	Proverbs 3:5-6	Proverbs 3:5-6
Wednesday	Psalm 9:7-10	Psalm 9:10
Thursday	Romans 8:28-30	Romans 8:28, 30
Friday	John 10:27-30	John 10:28-29

	READ	S.O.A.P.
WEEK 6	**YOU'RE INVITED**	
Monday	Romans 8:14-17	Romans 8:16-17
Tuesday	Hebrews 13:20-21	Hebrews 13:21
Wednesday	Jeremiah 29:11-13	Jeremiah 29:11
Thursday	2 Corinthians 12:9-10	2 Corinthians 12:9
Friday	Revelation 19:6-9	Revelation 19:9

	READ	S.O.A.P.
WEEK 7	**LOVING IS OUR KINGDOM WORK**	
Monday	1 John 4:16-21	1 John 4:19-21
Tuesday	1 Peter 4:8-11	1 Peter 4:8
Wednesday	John 13:34-35	John 13:34-35
Thursday	John 15:9-17	John 15:12-13
Friday	1 John 3:16-24	1 John 3:23-24

	READ	S.O.A.P.
WEEK 8	**LOVE AS A WAY OF LIFE**	
Monday	Matthew 22:36-40	Matthew 22:37-38
Tuesday	1 Corinthians 13:1-3	1 Corinthians 13:1-3
Wednesday	1 Corinthians 13:4-7	1 Corinthians 13:4-7
Thursday	1 Corinthians 13:8-13	1 Corinthians 13:8, 13
Friday	Leviticus 19:18	Leviticus 19:18

Goals

BEFORE YOU BEGIN working through the eight-week reading plan, we believe it's important that you write out goals. Take some time now and write three goals you would like to focus on as you begin to dig into God's Word. Be sure to refer back to these goals throughout the next eight weeks to help you stay focused. *You can do it!*

My goals for this session are:

1. to know that I am loved and lovable.

2.

3.

SIGNATURE: _____

DATE: _____

Week 1

Week 1 Challenge:

Do you live moment by moment, knowing that God loves you? Do you dwell in the security and assurance of His love, or is there a voice or obstacle that keeps you from knowing His love?

Write down your fears, failures, and faults on a piece of paper. Leave room at the top.

Then across the top of the paper write:

"While we were yet sinners, Christ died for us" (Romans 5:8). Nothing can separate me from the love of God. I cast all of these sins, failures, thoughts away, and accept His love forever and ever.

Finally, tear up your paper and throw it away. Let it be a physical representation of how God cast away your sin and replaced it with His love.

Week 1 Memory Verse:

*The L*ORD *your God is with you,*

   the Mighty Warrior who saves.

He will take great delight in you;

   in his love he will no longer rebuke you,

   but will rejoice over you with singing.

   Zephaniah 3:17, NIV

CHAPTER 1

He Calls Us Beloved

Sally

> *God's unfailing love for us is an objective fact affirmed over and over in the Scriptures. It is true whether we believe it or not. Our doubts do not destroy God's love, nor does our faith create it. It originates in the very nature of God, who is love, and it flows to us through our union with His beloved Son.*
>
> JERRY BRIDGES

AT THE AGE OF forty-two, after three miscarriages (including one during which I almost died and had to be rushed to the emergency room), I thought I would never have another child.

Then one day my son Nathan, a scruffy, loud, and always moving little boy, came to me and announced, "Mama, I sure do think you should have one more little baby, and it should be a little girl."

"Well, Nathan," I began, wrapping my arm around his little shoulders and pulling him close to me on the couch, "Mama's body is getting just a little bit old, and I haven't been able to have a baby for several years. Remember when I was in the hospital? Well, that was because I wasn't able to keep the sweet baby who was inside my 'tummy.'"

"But, Mama, you always tell us you believe in prayer. Are you willing to pray about it? Maybe God would do a miracle and give us one more little girl. You do believe God can do a miracle, don't you?"

So I prayed, and sure enough six weeks later, I was throwing up and had morning sickness for the next eight months!

During the last two months this baby was inside the womb, we prayed for a safe, healthy delivery. One of my friends would pat me on my belly as she prayed, and she would always call the baby Joy, since this little one was such an amazing miracle and an answer to the prayer for our family.

In fact, we did name our younger daughter Joy, and she ended up living up to her name. To our family she is a total joy. Perhaps because I never thought I would have a child again, I did not mind the sleepless nights, her cries, or her baby needs quite as much as I did as a younger mom.

Joy moved from a crib to a real bed when she was about two and a half years old. Often, at the crack of dawn she would climb next to me in my bed, squeezing and snuggling tightly against my body. After settling in, she would fall back asleep for a while longer.

Her feather-soft hair would tickle my cheek, and her warm pudgy body, soft to my skin, was a delight to me as I wrapped my arms around this tiny gift and held her tight.

"Mama," she said thoughtfully early one morning, "this is where I most belong, as close as I can get to you, because I can feel your love better when I am closer."

Then a smile crept across her little face as she breathed out a sigh and settled into a few more minutes of "love."

Because Joy was my beloved, prayed-for little girl, I loved having her next to me. I cherished the times I still had a little girl who wanted to be so near me, one who would trust me utterly. As her parent, I was so thankful she wanted to be near her mama. When she crawled into my bed and cuddled next to me, I was filled with happiness and appreciation of the gift she was to me. I loved it that she loved me! It didn't matter what she had done the day before—

> if she had cried a lot
> or broken a mug full of juice
> or fought with her brother
> or disobeyed me

She did not have to promise to be more mature, or confess her faults, or stay away because of having a bad day the day before.

At any time, she could just snuggle up next to me, because as my daughter, she belonged there! I delighted having her near me. She was my own little girl. I loved her with my whole heart, and I loved knowing that she wanted to be close to me and that she depended on me for her security, protection, comfort, and love.

My love for her had nothing to do with her performance. My love was committed, solid, and constant because she was my beloved one.

This is a human picture of God's parent love for us. The very nature of God is to love. He can do nothing else. His love defines Him, so His love for us is settled forever and cannot be changed.

Of course, we will never come close to the perfection or holiness of God. We are selfish most every day! We often say things that are harsh, do petty things, and act in a stingy or angry way. Yet still He loves us and wants us to be close to Him! It is almost impossible to believe that He could love us even when we are not loving to Him.

In the same way that I did not expect Joy to behave like an adult but accepted her limitations as a normal little toddler, so God is mindful of our own limitations and yet still loves us.

God sees us as toddlers, so to speak. Understanding our fragility, our humanness, He responds to us as I responded to Joy. He is mature even when we are not. He is constant in His love toward us, His commitment, His care for our needs, and His compassion for our heart's cry. As our heavenly Father, no matter what we do or how we fail Him, He is the constant one, the responsible one. He knows our frame—that we are weak, immature, and imperfect, but He doesn't require us to perform before we come close. He just wants our heart to trust Him, and He wants us to depend on Him as our loving Father.

When we come to Him as a child—innocent, dependent, trusting, and humble—He welcomes us into the place right next to His heart.

Even as an artist prefers his own art, or a musician his music, so God loves just exactly who we are because He made us this way. He loves His own artwork—us!

He formed us, gave us personality, knows our quirks, crafted our hair and eye color, our stature, our frame. Because we are His very own artwork and design, He takes pleasure in us and understands us as no one else does.

However, many of us spend our whole lives trying to earn the love of God because we think His love for us is based on works. We are a part of the family of God—and so we belong with Him. There is no special ticket, no need to earn or prove ourselves. For better or worse, we have His name, His love, His loyalty, His acceptance.

And because of this we can have hope. He said that He is going to build a place for us—a place to belong where we can celebrate even more in the beauty of His creation.

So often, we want to please God so we seek to keep a list of holy rules or behaviors.

We strive and work and fret in our Christian life to do "God's will."

The truth is, we cannot do the will of God until we know and experience the love of God.

As we accept and live within the sweet comfort and security He offers, we will find the strength to live our lives well in a fallen world.

We know our inheritance is sure and we are related to the King, which makes us royalty! Our heritage is beautiful, and we are in the company of all those who have accepted God's love and allowed themselves to be adopted by Him.

If this is true, then why do we not experience this intimate and secure comfort from God every day of our lives?

If we truly are as precious to Him as my precious little Joy is to me, then what is the barrier? Surely if God is willing to be that close and available to us, our lives should be different because of His love. People should see us filled with peace because we know that God will always be with us and protect us. We should feel secure and special, because we know how great His love is toward us every day.

The more we look into His heart and see His love, the more transformed we will become. We will be at peace, no longer having to work for our salvation. We will have humility, which will come out of gratitude and the desire to share this peace with others who so desperately need to know His love.

Perhaps there will be times when the selfish, immature toddler in us comes out, even as it did in Joy. We may tell ourselves

You eat too much.
You yell at your children.

You have committed sins that are too much even for
    God to overlook.
You are too lazy.
You make the same mistakes over and over again.
You complain and whine so much.
You are so selfish.

These messages in our head may be an accurate list of our own imperfections—but they do not define us. Jesus came while we were yet sinners to die for us—even before we asked. We did not deserve it then and we will never deserve it. It is not about "deserving"; it is about His great heart, His deep wellspring of abiding love, His commitment to our well-being throughout our lives.

Today, as you are, as He created you, with that body, that personality, that history, He loves you and considers you special because you are His! And He will redeem your story one day into a great love story with a happy ending—it is who He is; it is the promise He gave you when you were adopted by Him.

A person who feels loved lives with relief that she does not have to perform. She lives with joy knowing she is acceptable as she is. She lives with hope because she is not alone.

Reflection Questions

READ AND RESPOND TO the questions below in light of the verses that follow them. Each passage highlights something God says is true about His love for us:

1. *Do you realize that nothing you do will ever separate you from the love of God? How can you live into this truth? Even the dark moments of your life that seem to obscure Him from your eyes do not hide you from Him. He is with you always. Psalm 139 tells us that even the darkness is not dark to Him. He is your shepherd. He died for you. He wants to guide you, show you compassion, and show you mercy. He loves you, and you can never separate yourself from His love.*

   In all these things we are more than conquerors through him who loved us. For I am convinced that neither death nor life, neither angels nor demons, neither the present nor the future, nor any powers, neither height nor depth,

nor anything else in all creation, will be able to separate
us from the love of God that is in Christ Jesus our Lord.
Romans 8:37–39, NIV

nothing can separate me from the love of God

2. *What does it mean to you that God is a warrior big enough
to fight your battles? Imagine Him fighting for you today.
You must turn to Him and allow Him to lovingly guide you
and give you His love. Imagine Him singing over you out of
His delight. That is what we read, and it is true!*

The LORD your God is with you,

   the Mighty Warrior who saves.

He will take great delight in you;

   in his love he will no longer rebuke you,

but will rejoice over you with singing.

Zephaniah 3:17, NIV

*turn to God with my problems, my
fears, my doubts; He will fight for me.*

3. *There is only one one-word definition in Scripture about God—* <u>*God is love.*</u> *His very essence is love! And when you learn to accept that God's love for you is freely given, no matter what you do, you will begin to love others as He loves you—with grace, generosity, and without condemnation. Can you think of anyone in your life who needs to know this kind of love from you and from God?*

Dear friends, let us love one another, for love comes from God. Everyone who loves has been born of God and knows God. Whoever does not love does not know God, because God is love.

1 John 4:7-8, NIV

God is love

4. *What about when you blow it—again? You are impatient and yell at your children. You don't measure up to your ideals. How can you quickly restore your fellowship with God and others?*

   The verses below show us God's true nature—He has compassion on us in our weakness and difficulties on this earth. When we <u>turn our hearts to Him</u>, we will <u>find Him</u> to be slow to anger. No matter who else in our lives is impatient, <u>God is <u>patient</u>. He overflows with love and will always be there for us because He is faithful.</u>

You, Lord, are a compassionate and gracious God,

slow to anger, abounding in love and faithfulness.

Psalm 86:15, NIV

God is love. He is slow to anger and He is compassionate.

Prayer:

Dear Sweet Father, thank You for always loving me. Help me to come close to You, as a child to her mother, because You want to be my strength, help, comfort, and provider. Thank You that there is no limitation to Your love and that it will always be with me and guide me. In Jesus' sweet name I come!

Week 1: Monday

Read: Psalm 139

SOAP: Psalm 139:7-10

S   Write out the **Scripture** passage for the day.

O   Write down one or two **observations** from the passage.

- God encircles me. His hand is on me.
  - He is in complete control

- even the darkness is not dark to him

A   Write down one to two **applications** from the passage.

- I don't need to worry or be anxious. He is in control

- He will always be with me. He knows everything about me

P   **Pray** over what you learned from today's passage.

Week 1: Tuesday

Read: Romans 8:35-39

SOAP: Romans 8:37-39

S   Write out the **Scripture** passage for the day.

O   Write down one or two **observations** from the passage.

A   Write down one to two **applications** from the passage.

P   **Pray** over what you learned from today's passage.

Week 1: Wednesday

Read: Zephaniah 3:17

SOAP: Zephaniah 3:17

S Write out the **Scripture** passage for the day.

O Write down one or two **observations** from the passage.

A Write down one to two **applications** from the passage.

P **Pray** over what you learned from today's passage.

Week 1: Thursday

Read: Isaiah 43:1-7

SOAP: Isaiah 43:1, 4

S   Write out the **Scripture** passage for the day.

O   Write down one or two **observations** from the passage.

A   Write down one to two **applications** from the passage.

P   **Pray** over what you learned from today's passage.

Week 1: Friday

Read: Psalm 86:15

SOAP: Psalm 86:15

S Write out the **Scripture** passage for the day.

O Write down one or two **observations** from the passage.

A Write down one to two **applications** from the passage.

P **Pray** over what you learned from today's passage.

Week 2

Week 2 Challenge:

Write an action plan of how you are going to pursue God this week. When are you going to spend time in His Word and in prayer? How are you going to make time in your schedule to slow down so that you can just be still and listen?

Week 2 Memory Verse:

I will give them a heart to know me, that I am the LORD. They will be my people, and I will be their God, for they will return to me with all their heart.

Jeremiah 24:7, NIV

CHAPTER 2

Knowing God

Angela

AHHH, TO KNOW GOD. To really know Him. It would make all the difference in the world. If we truly knew Him, we would be braver, live more expectantly, and honor Him more with our lives. A proper perspective of our King of kings would cause us to live each day focused on Him, desiring to live more as He did, willing to let go of what this world offers—the houses, clothes, and material things—and instead reach for God. We would be willing to let go of our quest to "find ourselves" and truly focus on knowing Him. Knowing Him, the King of kings, the God of the universe, the Great I AM. But just how do we go about doing that?

I still remember the first day I saw my husband. It was at my eighth grade graduation, and he was standing in front of the whole class receiving an honor for getting all A's through middle school. I remember noticing him for two reasons: I never in a million years would be able to get all As, so that was quite an accomplishment to me, and I could not believe a guy could be so cute and smart at the same time. I was quite impressed!

I distinctly remember making a mental note that I would for

sure check him out later in high school. The year before my family had moved from California, so I was now attending middle school in Ohio. During seventh grade, I went to three different schools before my family finally settled down in the community in which I would spend my high school years. My seventh grade year was a blur, to say the least, and somehow I had missed knowing anything about this mysteriously handsome guy.

Our freshman year in high school came and went without me making good on my pledge. Let's just say we did not have any of the same classes, so we did not run into each other. Then in our sophomore year we somehow ended up having an art class together. I thought, *Maybe a brainiac and a nonbrainiac can at least have art in common—maybe.*

At that point all I knew about him was that his name was Dirk; he was in my grade and now in my art class; and he was as good-looking as ever. That was it—the complete sum of my knowledge of him at that time.

I think some of us approach God that way too. We know a lot about Him. We can state our facts, quote important verses, and have the main Bible stories memorized, but the relationship stops short of being personal. We don't know His heart or speak to Him as a friend.

At the time we started art class together, I had not spent any time with Dirk. I had only observed him from afar. I knew a few facts about him. From my friends, I learned that he had an older sister and a younger brother. My friends told me he had attended the same school since kindergarten. From studying him I could tell Dirk's style of dress and the sports he played. But it was all facts and no relationship.

Is that how you approach God? Do you know lots of important facts about Jesus—maybe where He was born and how old

He was when He died? What about His friends? Maybe you know their names and remember some of the stories Jesus told. But that's the kicker: Knowing a lot about someone doesn't mean you *know* him. It just means you know about him.

I would soon get to know Dirk better. It began with an invitation. After our art class God kept finding ways for Dirk and me to run into each other. First we were both selected to go on a special leadership retreat for school. Then we ended up together in the same computer class. Eventually we ended up spending more and more time together.

As God began developing our friendship, Dirk decided to call me at home one night to ask me a question. He wanted to know if I would like to go to the winter dance with him. Of course I responded with an excited yes, and our friendship went from being friends to liking each other to Dirk officially asking me to date him exclusively just a few months later. Each step along the path, our commitment grew stronger and stronger as we spent more time with each other.

Really getting to know each other took time. It took patience. It took hours of opening up and talking, being real and letting our guards down. Over the course of the next five and a half years, we spent hours investing in each other. We stayed up late talking on the phone until my mom said it was time to hang up. Then we spent hours writing notes to give each other the next day at school.

As high school ended and college began, we decided to go to nearby colleges so we could at least spend time together on the weekends, and, yes, occasionally we couldn't help but meet for dinner in the middle of the week. Even when life was busy, assignments were plentiful, and stress was high, we still made time for each other.

Getting to know Jesus takes time too. It takes changing the relationship from one in which you think *I can date anyone* to *I will only date You*. It's exclusive. Getting to know Jesus is also intentional. It is purposeful. To really develop a relationship with Him, you'll want to spend time with Him. You will want to commit to read the Bible, spend time in prayer talking to Him, and learn to put His words into action in your life. But how do you do that? I'm so glad you asked!

Five Ways to Get to Know Jesus

1. Spend time reading the Bible

You will get to know Jesus as you spend time reading the Bible. In 2 Timothy 3:16 we read, "All Scripture is God-breathed" (NIV), meaning it all comes directly from Him.

That's why it is important to make a commitment to be in God's Word. Given all the hustle and bustle in our lives, that means setting aside time in our busy schedules to spend time with the Great I AM. That may mean getting up early in the morning, rising before your children do and before the day begins. Or if you're often up in the middle of the night so you can feed an infant, because you work the night shift, or simply because you're a night owl, the best time to dig into God's Word may be during your children's nap time or in the evening when the house is quiet. Either way, the time of day is not as important as the daily discipline of reading God's Word.

Be intentional, set aside time to be in God's Word, have a plan of action to follow, and then commit to the plan. I promise your life will change the more you spend time with the Great I AM.

For me personally, one thing that has really helped is to place my Bible on my nightstand next to my bed before I go to sleep each night. In the morning, after I turn off my alarm, I can quickly grab my Bible and read it right there in bed. Either way I'm able to pray, read that day's Scripture verses, and interact with God's Word by writing out what I learned or what God showed me that morning. Some mornings after I read and pray, I head to the kitchen and spend more time digging into God's Word, writing out what I am learning. It really helps to have my Bible next to me when I wake up, allowing me to dig into God's Word first thing.

The world is constantly telling us what is important and what we should value, so it's vital to spend time reading God's Word. That is how the Lord speaks directly to us. I can't tell you how many times I have been struggling with a difficult situation, a heartbreak, or a disappointment when God comforted or counseled me directly through the verses I read during my quiet time with Him.

If you truly want to get to know God better, you will spend time reading the Bible because that is where you will find the direct words of God. There is no other book that has these precious, life-changing, all-powerful words, so it's worth making time in our busy lives to spend reading, meditating, and soaking up God's Word.

2. Spend time in prayer

We also develop our relationship with Jesus as we spend time in prayer with Him. Can you imagine what type of relationship you would have with someone with whom you never communicated? Think of praying as talking with Jesus. It really is as easy as that. You don't need to come to Him with big words or lofty prayers; Jesus just wants you to come to Him as you are. Be honest with

Him. Tell Him about your struggles and where you need help in your life. Tell Him about your hopes, your dreams, and your goals in life. I know it might seem strange, but He cares about all aspects of your life, not just the spiritual parts. There is never a prayer request that is too small or too big for Jesus. He loves you, and He loves when you come to Him in prayer (see Psalm 5:3).

When you pray, just be yourself. Remember that He is the one who made you. He loves you just as you are. If you have made some mistakes, confess them to Him and ask Him to forgive you. It's not as if He doesn't know about them already. We all make mistakes, but don't let them hold you back from approaching God and experiencing His love, grace, and forgiveness.

If you are struggling to approach Jesus in prayer, read Hebrews 4:15-16, NIV:

> *For we do not have a high priest who is unable to sympathize*
> *with our weaknesses, but we have one who has been tempted*
> *in every way, just as we are—yet he did not sin. Let us*
> *then approach God's throne of grace with confidence, so*
> *that we may receive mercy and find grace to help us in*
> *our time of need.*

I know sometimes it can be hard to read the Bible and understand what God is saying. In those times I simply ask God for help. In Proverbs 2:1-6 we see a mother instructing her son to make his heart ready for understanding. Before you open your Bible, pray and ask God to help you understand what you are about to read. Ask Him to open your eyes so that you can see the truth of His Word. Proverbs 2:1-2, 5 says, "My son, if you accept my words and store up my commands within you, turning your ear to wisdom and applying your heart to understanding . . . then you will understand the fear of the LORD and find the knowledge of God"(NIV).

Over the past few years I have begun praying for understanding and wisdom before I open my Bible to study. I ask God to help me understand what I am about to read. I ask Him to speak directly to me through His Word and help me to have a soft heart to hear and receive what He has for me that day.

Interacting with Jesus in that way through prayer, reading the Bible, and inviting Him to speak to you directly from the verses you are reading are vital as you begin deepening your relationship with Jesus and getting to know Him better.

3. Spend time learning to listen and be still

Be still. That is often a challenge these days with so many distractions around us filling our days. Whether it is our cell phones going off because of text messages, voice mails, alerts, and notifications, or because of our demanding schedules with appointments, assignments, meetings, and activities, all these distractions make it hard to truly slow down and be still. But in Psalm 46:10 God tells us, "Be still, and know that I am God" (NIV).

There is something about being still, quieting our spirits, our minds, and our bodies, that helps us focus on God. I have heard it said that God is a gentleman. He will not break down a door but rather will quietly knock at the door of our hearts, waiting for us to let Him inside. The problem is our lives are so busy and loud that many of us do not hear Him knocking. We do not yet know His voice well enough to distinguish it from all the other voices we hear in our heads. Making time to be still before the Lord is so important because it allows us to solely focus on Him, to expectantly wait upon Him, and to develop the discipline of just being still.

Even Jesus had times in His life when He went away to pray and just be with God. If Jesus needed to do that, then we do too. We see in Luke 22:39, 41 that Jesus went out "as usual" to the Mount of Olives to pray: "Jesus went out as usual to the Mount of Olives. . . . He withdrew about a stone's throw beyond them, [and] knelt down and prayed" (NIV).

The words *as usual* mean it was not a one-time occurrence. Jesus had a habit of going to that spot and seeking God. That particular night was very special because it was the evening Jesus would be betrayed by one of His close friends and handed over to the Romans, who would later crucify Him.

In verse 42 Jesus was wrestling with God's will for His life. Jesus was real with God. He did not hide the fact that He wanted God to remove the coming cup of suffering and see if there were another way to save the world from their sins without it costing His life. Yet as He prayed and sought God, He was still and listened to the Father. In the end He accepted God's will for His life and humbly died on the cross for our sins.

Learning to listen is such an important part of any relationship. Think back to when you were first dating your husband or getting to know a close friend. Remember all the hours you spent talking and listening to him or her? One of the most important acts of love you can do for someone you care about is to slow down, sit down, and give him or her your undivided attention by listening. Learn to shut out the noise, the distractions of your day, and come before the Lord as you pray, read His Word, and quiet yourself before Him. That is when you can hear His voice—when you purposefully sit and listen.

God created us for rest. He even rested on the seventh day after He created the world. Why do we think we can constantly be on the go and not take time in our busy lives to just sit and be still?

4. Spend time in His creation

"Since the creation of the world God's invisible qualities—his eternal power and divine nature—have been clearly seen, being understood from what has been made, so that men are without excuse" (Romans 1:20, NIV). God's creation helps us to know God. He purposely designed His world that way. But many of us, especially in the United States, don't get out into God's creation enough to see Him in it. There is a difference between cognitively learning about what the ocean is like and actually experiencing its power and majesty.

I wanted my girls to learn this powerful lesson during a family vacation. As our rental car pulled into the overly crowded parking lot, which was filled with families unloading beach bags crammed full with sand toys, sunscreen, snacks, and plenty of water, my girls squealed, "We're finally here! The ocean! We finally get to see the ocean!" Mind you, we had just spent three days at Disneyland, but you would never have guessed it because they were brimming with excitement to get their little four- and five-year-old toes into the warm, soft sand. As we opened our minivan doors to join the other families for the day's excursion, we were welcomed by the sounds of seagulls flying above and greeted softly by the ocean breeze as it quickly blew through our van and then was gone.

I had brought my girls to the ocean because I wanted them to see God's beauty and His power and to experience what He had created. I wanted them to experience their God in a much bigger way. Being at the ocean does that. The beauty of the roaring, white-crested waves does that. The sound of the ocean waves roaring to shore, the soft breeze touching your face, and the birds singing above all testify to God's reality and greatness.

As we walked the beach picking up seashells, I talked to Paige and Addie about how wonderful and powerful our God is. We talked about how beautiful and unique each seashell they picked up was. We talked about God's creativity, about the size of the ocean and the power of the waves. I wanted them to see God in His creation. I wanted to be intentional and give them an opportunity to experience God in a whole new way and to open their eyes to the bigness of their God.

> *When we take the opportunity to expose our children to the glory of God displayed in a rainbow or powerful ocean waves or a star-studded night sky, we are helping them understand that there is a Being much bigger than themselves who created the universe and holds it together with His power. When we tell them about our answered prayers and those amazing "coincidences" that confirm God's presence in our lives, we help them realize that God is close and caring and active in our daily circumstances.*
>
> SALLY CLARKSON, *Ministry of Motherhood*

5. Come to Him as a child

Jesus said in Matthew 18:2-4 that unless we come to Him as a child, we will never really know Him. But how does a child come to God?

Sitting on the hard, wooden oak bench in our little church in Salt Lake City, Utah, I remember responding to an invitation one sunny Sunday morning at the church my family went to when I was around three years old. All I can remember from that special Sunday morning is the unexplainable love I felt for God. I wanted to be with Him, and I wanted Him to know how much I loved Him.

In my three-year-old mind, I thought the best way to let God know how much I loved Him was to be brave and walk up to the front of the church and let my pastor know that I loved Jesus. So I did. I was completely abandoned for God at the tender age of three. I wanted all of Him, and I wanted Him to have all of me. I was sold out. I knew He loved me because I believed what my mom had taught me, and I knew I loved Jesus, and that was all that mattered.

I had no theology alignments. No Bible verses memorized. I didn't even know what the Ten Commandments were, but it didn't matter at that stage in my life. I came to Jesus that morning just as I was, probably with milk spilled on my Sunday dress and maybe even wearing unmatched socks, but it didn't matter. I came anyway, just as I was. I didn't wonder what others thought. I don't think I could have even cared about something so trivial at that age. I came to Jesus as a response to love. I loved Him, and I wanted Him to know. That was it, plain and simple. I didn't want anything in return. There was no hidden agenda.

I think that is how God wants us to approach Him too. Actually I *know* that is how He wants us to approach Him. No agendas. Just love.

Getting to know God is very similar to getting to know a new friend or a future spouse. It takes time. It takes commitment. It takes investment. And sometimes the relationship deepens and matures through hard times. For me personally, college was a very hard time in my life. Because of circumstances out of my control, I felt at times as if I was going through the valley of the shadow of death. Yet because of those hard years, my relationship with Dirk only got stronger. He went through those tough times with me. He hurt for me when I was hurting. He did not run away from our relationship when things became hard. In fact, his commitment to me actually grew stronger during those dark times. And because of those I'm-tempted-to-give-up days, we both emerged stronger.

Looking back over those years, I'm grateful for those hard early times we weathered by clinging together, because it was in the stormy times that the roots of our relationship dug down deeper into God's abundantly rich soil. It was during those trying years, the years of tears, broken dreams, and heartache, that we learned to turn to God and to each other to find strength.

Our relationship with God can be a lot like that too. Sometimes it is through the hard "stuff," the hard years, that we truly develop our relationship with God. We learn to be broken before Him. Sometimes when we get to the place where He is all we have, we find that He is all we really need. These can be painful years, but precious years as well.

Knowing God may sound complicated and mysterious, but it really isn't. He has already wired you with the ability to do it. Just reach out to Him as you would a friend. All great relationships have a starting place. Be honest when you pray, read His Word, make time to spend with Him in your busy life, and get out and enjoy the beautiful world He created.

It's not as complicated as you might think; even kids can do it.

Reflection Questions

1. *In 2 Timothy 3:16 (NIV), we read that all Scripture is God-breathed. Knowing this truth, why is it so important to make sure we are reading God's Word on a daily basis for ourselves?*

2. *Read Hebrews 4:15-16. How does knowing that Jesus can sympathize with your weakness and relate to your temptations help you approach Him in prayer?*

3. *How does it change your outlook on God when you realize that He extends mercy and grace to us when we approach Him?*

4. *What are some ways you can choose to slow down your life so that you can "be still" before our Lord?*

5. *What are some ways that you "experience" God? For my husband, Dirk, it is when he is outside running. For me, it is when I'm reading His Word or rocking my children before bedtime. The wonderful thing is that God has created us all differently, so there is no right or wrong answer. He has wired us all to know Him, but some of us draw closer to Him through nature, others through worship, others through service, and the list goes on.*

6. *What do you think Jesus meant when He said we must come to Him as a child? What does that look like for you?*

7. *As you consider the different ways we can get to know God outlined in this chapter, name one or two areas on which you need to focus.*

Prayer:

Dear Lord, help us to know You better. Open our eyes to Your truth as we read Your loving Words. Help us to see You in Your creation and feel Your presence in our everyday lives. Help us to draw near to You, especially on days when it is hard to do. Amen.

Week 2: Monday

Read: Ephesians 1:17–19

SOAP: Ephesians 1:17–19

S   Write out the **Scripture** passage for the day.

O   Write down one or two **observations** from the passage.

A   Write down one or two **applications** from the passage.

P   Pray over what you learned from today's passage.

Week 2: Tuesday

Read: Colossians 1:9-14

SOAP: Colossians 1:9-10

S   Write out the **Scripture** passage for the day.

O   Write down one or two **observations** from the passage.

A   Write down one or two **applications** from the passage.

P   **Pray** over what you learned from today's passage.

Week 2: Wednesday

Read: Jeremiah 24:6-7

SOAP: Jeremiah 24:7

S   Write out the **Scripture** passage for the day.

O   Write down one or two **observations** from the passage.

A   Write down one or two **applications** from the passage.

P   **Pray** over what you learned from today's passage.

Week 2: Thursday

Read: 1 John 5:20

SOAP: 1 John 5:20

S   Write out the **Scripture** passage for the day.

O   Write down one or two **observations** from the passage.

A   Write down one or two **applications** from the passage.

P   **Pray** over what you learned from today's passage.

Week 2: Friday

Read: Jeremiah 31:33-34

SOAP: Jeremiah 31:33-34

S Write out the **Scripture** passage for the day.

O Write down one or two **observations** from the passage.

A Write down one or two **applications** from the passage.

P **Pray** over what you learned from today's passage.

Week 3

Week 3 Challenge:

Each of us carries in our minds the voices of others that accuse us of our inadequacies or failures over the years. Sometimes without even knowing it, we live under guilt or accusations. Examine your mind and heart and see if you are carrying voices that are not true. Satan would just love for you to walk with these lies weighing you down.

To demolish something means to totally destroy it. God wants you to destroy those thoughts that denounce you and that keep you from living in the freedom of His love.

Write down the lie you repeat in your head or the inadequacy that you feel. Now make a plan to capture the voice or thought every time it crosses your mind and to replace it with the memory verse below:

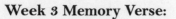

Week 3 Memory Verse:

Be alert and of sober mind. Your enemy the devil prowls around like a roaring lion looking for someone to devour.

1 Peter 5:8, NIV

CHAPTER 3

The Rival

*Satan Wants to Steal and Destroy Our Confidence
in God's Unchanging Love*

> *Be alert and of sober mind. Your enemy the devil prowls around like a roaring
> lion looking for someone to devour.* 1 PETER 5:8, NIV

HEAVY, SWEET SCENTS pervaded the air of the old, vine-covered
Mexican villa as I walked through the garden and breathed in the
perfumed air. As a young college student, adventure, new experiences, and exploring new places seemed like a gift! Attending a
Christian summer conference for students in a charming hotel in
Guadalajara, Mexico, presented just the opportunity my friend
and I were looking for.

At first I felt encouraged as I met with articulate students and
interesting professors and learned about the Bible in depth for
the very first time as a new Christian. However, with every day,
a shadow seemed to creep more profoundly over my heart.

A realization that "I was not worthy," that I was inadequate
before God, weighed like a ton of bricks on my heart. I smiled
on the outside and performed the tasks of living with these new

friends as best I could. But no one could have guessed what the voices were saying to me inside my mind.

Without even noticing, I had been gathering a bundle of guilt and inadequacy that I carried every day. My failures, my inadequacy, and my fears were a dark cloud that I carried and that often defined how I felt about myself.

You are not loved because you are inadequate. You are just playing the role of being a Christian, but God is disappointed in you. If people knew what you are really like, they would see your shame and shortcomings.

I must interrupt my story. I must ask you, the reader: What voices are you listening to in your own mind or heart? Is it that of a mother or father who humiliated you? A husband who shows his anger? Have you done something you consider terrible that you feel will mar you forever?

Well, that is how I felt. And until you give these voices up to God, you will never truly enjoy the fun in life, the blessing of His favor, or the true warmth of His love.

. Back to my story.

Clamoring voices demoralized me as I ambled down the shadowy hallway toward a meeting with a total stranger, one of the instructors who had offered to meet with me. *You shouldn't admit out loud that you feel unloved and lonely,* I thought. *That will sound pathetic, whiny. Perhaps this man will see that you deserve to be rejected for all the imperfections of your life, the ways you can never live up to your own standards. He won't understand. No one does.*

At twenty years old, I wore a mask of friendliness, a facade that people observed but that did not resemble my inside feelings. I tried and tried to make myself as perfect as possible, hoping someone would truly love me. I attempted to win favor by my looks, including my long, blonde hair, by my performance at school, and by all things external. Perhaps on the outside, I looked like I had it all together, but on the inside I was crumbling. I felt too unworthy for anyone to love me.

Two nights before my meeting with the instructor, I had slumped alone under my covers, weeping desperately and physically aching as though something inside was going to burst. No matter what I accomplished or how hard I attempted to be excellent, I always fell short. A deep longing to be known and still loved haunted me daily.

Too young to understand, I had not realized that somehow, I had received a message from my family and the world that their love was based on my performance. My friends seemed to say the same thing—if I did the right things, I would be acceptable. If I pleased them, I would be popular, but if they saw the real me, they would not want to know me. If I made a mistake or chose different values, I would be ignored or condemned.

Love had been conditional, based on my performance, and I never knew when I was going to be "in" or "out," accepted or rejected. I had been surrounded by those who felt free to criticize me, and I had listened to their messages.

I had been seeking the impossible. I had been striving my whole life to be enough to impress my family, to affirm the longings in my heart to be noticed, heard, understood, and loved for who I was as I was. All I wanted was to curl up in the arms of someone strong who would truly love me. I wanted to find the comfort and security I had always longed for but never quite experienced. But I would never admit that out loud!

Because I'd felt so joyful when I first became a Christian, I was surprised at the amount of conflict I was feeling inside. And so, my Bible professor had agreed to meet with me and discuss my questions. Of course, now that I was heading toward the evening meeting with him, I questioned myself and hoped no one would see me. But still I went and hoped for some answers.

As I poured out my heart to this instructor whom I barely knew, he looked me in the eyes with compassion, gentleness, and love—there was no condemnation there.

"Sally, I understand everything you are feeling. We all feel inadequate because without the love and forgiveness of God, we spend our whole lives trying to do enough good deeds to earn His love. Your parents were not a good representation of God; they made you feel further condemned because their approval was based on your performance.

"But you are listening to the old voices. God is so excited that you put your faith in Him. Do you think that, now that you are a child of His, He would try to discourage you in your faith?

"The truth is, you will never have to perform for God, because His love for you is endless, infinite, constant, and abundant once you put your faith in Him.

"But I want you to look at me and listen. There is one who wants to keep you from knowing the amazing love of God— Satan despises those who want to love God. He would love to whisper words of darkness into your heart so that you will be distracted and waste your time trying to please God, when you are already all that you need to be to please Him.

"You must begin to recognize the voices that are not truth and then determine not to accept them as truth or listen to them. All you have to do is reject Satan's lies and live into the truth and strong foundations of love that God has communicated to you in Scripture! There will always be a spiritual battle going on in your heart, because Satan comes to steal your faith and confidence.

"But this is what you must know: In John 10:10, Jesus said, 'The thief [Satan] comes only to steal and kill and destroy.'

"The devil lied to Adam and Eve in the garden.

"He accuses us before God day and night. Revelation 12:10 says, 'The accuser of our brethren has been thrown down, he who accuses them before our God day and night.'

"Satan knows that if he can get you to focus on yourself and look at your inadequacies, you will not be free to enjoy the incredible love and forgiveness of God. When you listen to his voice, you are actually giving into Satan's lies and then he has you living a defeated life.

"So the more mature you become, the more you will discern God's voice from the voice of Satan or others whom you have listened to before now. You don't have to live by these voices any more. In 2 Corinthians 5:17, the apostle Paul says you are a new creature in Christ—brand-new with a new start."

Then my instructor told me, "Sally, I want you to know these truths:

"You are beloved. 'To all . . . who are loved by God and called to be his holy people: Grace and peace to you from God our Father and from the Lord Jesus Christ' (Romans 1:7, NIV).

"You are God's princess. 'You are a chosen people, a royal priesthood, a holy nation, God's special possession, that you may declare the praises of him who called you out of darkness into his wonderful light' (1 Peter 2:9, NIV).

"You are royalty because you have been adopted by the King, the creator of the universe. That is your heritage and that is the reality of His love for you," this wise man spoke to me with such gentleness of voice.

"But you must write all of your inadequacies out on a paper

with me right now—all of your fears and failures and the messages of accusations that float around in your mind."

And so I did. I poured out my thoughts on paper while he waited quietly.

When I stopped, he took the paper and began to write across the top.

Therefore, there is now no condemnation for Sally who is in Christ Jesus.
(SEE ROMANS 8:1, NIV)

Sally, God does not condemn you.

I am convinced that neither death nor life, neither angels nor demons, neither the present nor the future, nor any powers, neither height nor depth, nor anything else in all creation, will be able to separate Sally from the love of God that is in Christ Jesus our Lord.
(SEE ROMANS 8:38-39, NIV)

Sally, nothing you can ever do will separate you from God's love. He will always and always love you.

As far as the east is from the west,
So far has He removed our transgressions from us.
PSALM 103:12

God has removed all of Sally's sins and failures away from her so that she will never ever have to see them again!

The LORD's lovingkindnesses indeed never cease,
For His compassions never fail.
They are new every morning;
Great is Your faithfulness.
LAMENTATIONS 3:22-23

Then he looked up at me and asked, "Sally, did you know that the loving-kindness of God toward you will never, ever come to an end? That He understands you and has compassion for your struggles? That His loving-kindness will be new and fresh for you every day? God will always be faithful to you.

"All these things I am telling you today are true about you. But you have to live in the truth and not live in the lies that accuse you in your mind. You must, as a little girl before God, run to Him with open arms and rest and abide in this great love. Only when you accept this love and trust Him will you ever be free from the darkness you feel.

"Now we have written these truths across all of your confessions. I want you to give all of your failures and sins and shortcomings into the hands of God and leave them there. You must never, ever let these define you again, because you are forgiven, loved, cherished, redeemed, and adopted by God.

"Are you ready to believe He loves you?"

This act of writing down the messages from the negative voices inside and then tearing up the list gave me a feeling of ridding myself from them forever. But even more, understanding that God's voices for me would be love, instruction, encouragement, and not condemnation changed my life forever. It didn't happen all at once— it took me a while to rid myself of them completely, but little by little, I lived into God's love, and it gave me such great joy and freedom to be myself—to not have to perform for anyone anymore.

And so, I ask you, sweet friend, as you read this chapter today, will you believe the lies of Satan, or will you accept God's love and your immense value to Him? He loves your eye color, your shyness or enthusiastic personality, your shortness or muscular body—He delights in you as you are now, because He made you to have joy, happiness, and fullness of life! Your secure position as His royal one with a possession and inheritance waiting for you will be revealed to you in heaven—and I can tell you, it will be grand.

Most women are very deep of feeling and are very susceptible to moods and especially to living in guilt, fear, or inadequacy. Our feelings are a gift from God. Our feelings of love, compassion, mercy, sympathy, and tenderness are a part of our glory as women. When we exercise our feelings of love toward those whom God has brought into our lives, we bring great encouragement and strength to others—our friends, children, husband, acquaintances.

But as deeply emotional beings, we are also very susceptible to feelings of guilt, inadequacy, and insecurity. These negative feelings can grip us and take a stronghold on our hearts. They can keep us captive to the dark voices we often hear, either from others who have wrongly influenced our lives or from our own feelings of failure.

First, we need to recognize that being a great lover is one of the best accomplishments we can attain and it makes us most like Christ. Loving generously and deeply is a beautiful mantle for a woman to wear. Jesus said that Christians would be truly known in the world by our love—unconditional, redeeming love for one another.

We must understand that Satan, the archenemy of God, knows how very powerful the love of Christ through us can be. He would do almost anything to keep us from understanding our great value to God so that he can cripple us. Satan just hates for us to know that we are anointed with favor from a God who delights in using normal people to accomplish great things. He whispers to us that we are not worthy in hopes that he can keep us from living a story worth telling through the days of our lives!

We cannot be free to love as long as we are dwelling on ourselves—our own inadequacies, bitterness, or lack of forgiveness for ourselves or for others. Jesus desires us to live freely, with no condemnation hanging over our heads, so that we become freer to love others well.

How freeing to begin to understand that we do not have to wear the guilt or heaviness of the mantle of Satan's accusations. Our precious Father wants us to understand the battle waged against us so we are not victims.

Looking back at the story of the kind ways He began to reveal His love for me is sweet to remember. My story above tells about the beginning of my living into becoming a loved one. The more I was free to enjoy His love, the more I was free to confidently begin sharing His love, His design, and His messages, spreading His influence through my life to others.

Reflection Questions

1. *What voices are in your heart and head that accuse you and belittle you? Write down the messages you have been listening to, and then write 1 John 1:9 across the top of the page: "If we confess our sins, He is faithful and righteous to forgive us our sins and to cleanse us from all unrighteousness."*

2. *How does our world try to make women measure ourselves by external factors—clothing, performance, personality, looks— instead of valuing us for who God made us to be?*

3. *Do you understand that loving yourself is a part of your spiritual worship of God? What do you need to address in your life so that you will love yourself as you are?*

4. *Are there any patterns of thinking that your family gave to you while growing up that need to be replaced with God's voice? What verses can you find that can become God's voice to you when you catch yourself listening to those negative voices?*

5. *How can you use what you have learned to be a bridge to the lives of other women? Often, out of the lessons we have learned through our mistakes and failures, we receive the most profound messages for other women. How can God cause all things to work together for good in your own life (see Romans 8:28)?*

Prayer:

Dear Precious Lord, thank You that You see me as a new creature in Christ. I am as innocent as a little child in Your eyes. I can live as a beloved one, free from the burdens of this broken world, because You will always see me through the eyes of Jesus, my forever lover and Redeemer. I am so very grateful that my failures do not define me in Your estimation, but that Your inheritance and calling are beautiful. I love You and am so very grateful to You.

I come humbly to You in the precious name of Jesus.

Week 3: Monday

Read: 1 Peter 5:6-9

SOAP: 1 Peter 5:8

S Write out the **Scripture** passage for the day.

O Write down one or two **observations** from the passage.

A Write down one or two **applications** from the passage.

P **Pray** over what you learned from today's passage.

Week 3: Tuesday

Read: Revelation 12:10-12

SOAP: Revelation 12:10

S   Write out the **Scripture** passage for the day.

O   Write down one or two **observations** from the passage.

A   Write down one or two **applications** from the passage.

P   **Pray** over what you learned from today's passage.

Week 3: Wednesday

Read: Romans 8:1-4

SOAP: Romans 8:1

S   Write out the **Scripture** passage for the day.

O   Write down one or two **observations** from the passage.

A   Write down one or two **applications** from the passage.

P   **Pray** over what you learned from today's passage.

Week 3: Thursday

Read: 1 Peter 2:9

SOAP: 1 Peter 2:9

S   Write out the **Scripture** passage for the day.

O   Write down one or two **observations** from the passage.

A   Write down one or two **applications** from the passage.

P   **Pray** over what you learned from today's passage.

Week 3: Friday

Read: Lamentations 3:22-23

SOAP: Lamentations 3:22-23

S Write out the **Scripture** passage for the day.

O Write down one or two **observations** from the passage.

A Write down one or two **applications** from the passage.

P **Pray** over what you learned from today's passage.

Week 4

Week 4 Challenge:

In one of his letters to a first-century church, the apostle Paul talks about an unspecified difficulty, which he calls "a thorn in my flesh":

> *Three times I pleaded with the Lord to take it away from me. But he said to me, "My grace is sufficient for you, for my power is made perfect in weakness." Therefore I will boast all the more gladly about my weaknesses, so that Christ's power may rest on me.*
> 2 CORINTHIANS 12:8-9, NIV

I know this may be hard for you, but I want you to focus on thanking God for a specific challenge in your own life, which may feel like a persistent thorn stuck in your flesh. Pray and ask Him this week for help to see the purpose in it and how you can bring glory to God because of it. Ask Him to use the pain that this difficulty has caused to bring good and healing.

This week write a letter to God thanking Him for the thorn in your life, focusing on the good it brings into your life. For me, my thorn makes me cling to Jesus because I know I can't do anything without Him. My thorn keeps me humble and reminds me of my dependence on God. Because of it I also know God can work powerfully through people's lives if they are willing to be obedient to His calling on their lives and submit to His will.

Week 4 Memory Verse:

Because of his great love for us, God, who is rich in mercy, made us alive with Christ even when we were dead in transgressions—it is by grace you have been saved.

Ephesians 2:4-5, NIV

CHAPTER 4

God Loves You

Angela

YOU ARE LOVED.

Not because you get straight As or don't get straight As
   in school.
You are loved.

Not because of your athletic abilities or lack thereof.
You are loved.

Not because of the good things you have done, or because
   of your past.
You are loved because you are His.

When you accept Jesus Christ as Savior of your life and invite Him into your heart, you are His. And He loves you just as you are, the way He made you. Never forget that.

You are His masterpiece, and when He looks at you, He sees perfection. He sees a princess. I know this can be hard to understand and even harder to really let seep into your soul, but just rest in this truth right now. You are loved, not because of what you have done, but because of Whose you are. You are His.

I know from personal experience that this is a hard truth to understand. I remember when I first started dating my husband I would get nervous and not want him to get to know me too well. I was afraid he would find out how boring I was and decide to leave me. So I made up my mind to remain mysterious, as if a high school girl can even be mysterious.

I remember that as Dirk was driving us somewhere on a date, he would begin to ask me questions about my childhood—my likes, my dislikes—and I would answer them to a point and then stop. I didn't want him to get too close; I knew I couldn't stand the rejection, so I held him at arm's length for a while. Yet Dirk was determined to get to know me and not just stay on the surface level of shallow, empty conversations.

Because I wasn't happy with the way God had made me, I could not understand someone else being okay with it. I felt broken. I felt boring, and it made my hopeful heart sink. I felt as if God had made a mistake when He made me, and I did not want anyone to know, so I tried my best to cover it up and to hide.

From the outside no one could see the inner turmoil I went through on a daily basis. I felt as Paul did in 2 Corinthians 12:7 when he talked about his thorn in the flesh. I, too, have a "thorn," and I've begged God to remove it from me for years. In my limited understanding of God's plan for my life, I was sure He had accidentally made a mistake when He made me. If only He could change this one thing about me, I knew I could serve Him much better.

I struggled a lot with learning to read in elementary school. To this day I remember being in kindergarten and one of my classmates knowing how to read on the first day of school. I remember the little girl sitting in front of us in the teacher's chair the very first morning of school and reading a book to the whole class. I sat astonished that she could conquer that amazing feat, and I recall the sickening feeling in my stomach because I didn't think I ever could.

I remember becoming frustrated that same year in kindergarten because I was having trouble remembering how to spell my last name and fitting my twelve-letter last name onto the page. So I kept erasing it and starting over again. My poor kindergarten teacher got so tired of waiting for me to finish an assignment that she finally cut off all my erasers so I couldn't erase another letter if I made a mistake. I just had to move on. That was devastating to me.

In first grade I realized I was not reading as well as my friends, and I became embarrassed. I hated having to read in front of my peers, so I started feeling sick when I had to go to school. A few months into first grade, I was tested and diagnosed as being "learning disabled." As I write this book, only my closest core group of friends even knows this about me. To this day I still struggle with that truth. Yet I'm learning as I mature in my faith that even with this thorn, this pain, I can still choose to give glory to God. Oh, how many tears have I cried, asking God why He has allowed this struggle into my life. I have to deal with its effects on a daily basis, yet if knowing this about me encourages one fellow sister in Christ to live more boldly and bravely for God, it is all worth it.

My life is for God's glory. I have questioned Him many times and even claimed that, if only He had made me without this thorn, I could change the world for Him! But He gently reminds me that I already am changing the world for His glory in just the way He had planned: through my weakness. With every blog post I write I have to depend on Him. With trembling hands and a nervous stomach I press "publish," hoping that what I wrote sounds okay, hoping that I didn't misspell a word, praying that the words He wrote through me touch at least one woman's heart and that she falls more in love with Him because of it.

By the time my senior year came around, Dirk and I had grown in our commitment to each other, so we began talking about either going away to different colleges or staying nearby. Dirk was applying to Ivy League schools, and I was just hoping to go to one nearby.

After one particular date in the spring of our senior year, I finally couldn't take it anymore. I broke down and told Dirk about my learning disability. We had been dating for almost a year by that time, and it was at the end of that particular date, while we were sitting at a picnic table at a park close to Dirk's house, when I finally couldn't keep my secret inside any longer. He needed to know that this girl he thought was so perfect really was broken. He didn't realize that every time I wrote him a note at home, I would write a rough draft or two before I actually gave it to him. No, I had hidden this secret from him for over a year because I was afraid once he knew how broken I was, he would leave. But I couldn't stand the hiding any longer, so the truth needed to come out.

That night, sitting on a park bench with tears streaming down my face, I let him know how broken I was, how I struggled where he never did. I told him of my painful childhood memories as I daily had to leave my classroom to go to the "special" class so I could get the help and support I needed. I feared his response. Would he be disappointed in me? Would my fear come true and he would leave me because I didn't meet his expectations?

That night on the park bench God used my boyfriend to begin healing the wounds of my childhood pain. The truth about me didn't change how Dirk viewed me or loved me. If anything, he fell more in love with me because I'd allowed myself to finally tear down the wall I had built around my heart, trying to protect myself from further pain or rejection. I felt as if I had lived a life with constant accusers telling me how stupid I was. I was tired of listening to how I would not amount to anything if everyone knew the real truth about me. Once I opened up and shared my truth, those voices were finally silenced.

One of my favorite stories in the Bible is found in John 8. It is the story about Jesus forgiving the adulterous woman. The teachers of the law and the Pharisees brought a woman to the feet of Jesus. They demanded that Jesus deal with her because of her great sin. Yet Jesus chose to extend grace and mercy to her instead, lifting her head and speaking words of encouragement and love over her. That's how I felt that night. Though the pain I had experienced was not due to any sin in my life, the result was the same. I felt unworthy, shameful, and broken, and I needed someone to speak words of encouragement, love, and grace into my life.

That evening was a turning point in my life. I was finally brave enough to let Dirk see the hurt and pain I had been carrying for years, and when he did, he responded lovingly. I learned that night that I don't have to be perfect to be loved and accepted by another person.

I have chosen to share this very personal and private story with you, sweet sister, with the hope that you, too, will see that you don't have to be perfect to be perfectly loved by God. Christ can be glorified through your weaknesses, if only you let Him. Now when I read 2 Corinthians 12:10—"When I am weak, then

I am strong"—I see the purpose in the pain. Though I cannot go as far as to say I'm thankful for my thorn, I do realize that it keeps me humble and reminds me that it is Christ who is doing the mighty work in and through me. I don't have to be perfect to be used mightily by my Lord.

With Jesus' help, we can silence the voices that tell us we have to be perfect to be loved by Him. Say this with me: "I don't have to be perfect to be perfectly loved by Jesus." Great; now say it again and again. Let those words take root in your precious heart. You might even want to write them out and place them on the mirror where you get ready in the morning. Remember, you don't have to be perfect to be loved by the One who is.

Embrace Who You Are

God knows your likes and dislikes. He made you with that exact personality, so use it and all the strengths that go with it for His glory. If you are strong-willed, then be strong-willed for Jesus and fight for justice. Fight for those who can't fight for themselves (Proverbs 31:8). Fight for what's right in the eyes of the Lord (Deuteronomy 6:18). If you are an encourager, then please use your gift to lift up the body of Christ. We need you! Bless those around you. When you think of an encouraging word, say it to someone. Don't hold it in but give him or her the gift of your kind words. We live in a day when so many people are discouraged, and what a soothing salve your words can be to their souls.

Embrace how God made you. Don't forget that the One who made delicate and intricate flowers, breathtaking mountain ranges, and glorious sunrises carefully designed you. The One who placed the stars in the sky and put the earth into motion made you. You are not a mistake, and neither is the way you are made. God saw you in your mother's womb (Psalm 139:13), and He has been crazy about you ever since.

It wasn't until I became a mother myself that I began to understand how crazy God is about His children. For me, every morning is like Christmas morning when I see my children. I am simply crazy about them! I can't wait to get them into my arms, to hug them, to kiss their sweet little cheeks and tell them that they are loved. The simple act of watching them sleep brings me so much joy, and yet they really are not doing anything. I love simply looking at them, watching them enjoy an ice cream cone or play outside with their friends. I take great delight in helping them learn how to color, read, or ride their bikes.

As a parent I understand that they are not going to do any of those things perfectly the first time. They are going to make mistakes. They are going to "color outside the lines." They are going to fall off their bikes, hurt themselves, and want to quit. But just as a loving mother comes alongside her children to help them learn and grow, encouraging them to press on through the hard times and not give up, God lovingly does that with us. He picks us up when we have fallen down. He brushes off the dirt, washes our clothes, and gives us another new, clean garment to wear.

Of course there are times in our lives when we will need to be disciplined by God because of our willful disobedience, but the Bible tells us that it is because of His love for us that He reprimands us (Proverbs 3:11-12). God disciplines those He loves because, like any good parent, He loves us and wants us to grow in godliness and maturity. Sometimes the path to maturity means we have to walk down some rough roads. But the wonderful thing about God is, when we walk with Him, we never walk alone. He is always right beside us, loving us, encouraging us, and helping us, even when we do not see it or feel it, just as any good and loving parent does.

Embrace Your Imperfection

We must accept the fact we are not perfect and never will be. Some days I have to remind myself of that truth over and over again. Much of our society today makes us feel that we, as women, moms, daughters, and even little girls, need to portray an image of perfection. But that was never God's intent. We can't turn on the TV or read a magazine in line at the grocery store without being told that lie through the Photoshop-corrected advertisements, articles, and commercials. But I am not a perfect woman. I am not a perfect wife, and I'm most definitely not a perfect mom. I struggle against my own expectations and those put on me by others and society in general. I struggle against my feelings of just not being enough—

> good enough
> smart enough
> funny enough
> entertaining enough
> kind enough
> intentional enough.
> enough, enough, enough . . .

But the older I become, the more I realize that I can't be enough. I'm going to make mistakes as I strive to be like Jesus each day. Unfortunately, I'm going to fail at goals I set; that's just a fact. Everyone wants to go through life making all the right decisions, never failing at anything, never disappointing anyone. But let me suggest that it is okay not to be perfect. And let me go a little further and say that it is okay for our children and others around us to see us as imperfect.

It is in those opportunities that we have the freedom to teach our children and those around us about grace. We need to teach them that God doesn't expect Mommy and Daddy to be perfect, just as God doesn't expect them to be perfect either. Mommy's and Daddy's love does not go away when they mess up, and neither does God's. It is so important to release them from the burden of having to be perfect. That burden is too heavy; it drains one's energy and zest for life. Please realize that God does not put that burden upon our shoulders; we do.

In Matthew 11:28-29 Jesus says, "Come to me, all you who are weary and burdened, and I will give you rest. . . . For I am gentle and humble in heart, and you will find rest for your souls" (NIV). Jesus does not want perfection from our children or from us. He wants a relationship, and relationships are not perfect. We see in all the great stories of the Bible that no one other than Jesus lived a perfect life.

David wasn't perfect, even though he was described as being a man after God's own heart. No, David was also an adulterer and murderer.

Peter wasn't perfect. Though he was zealous for Jesus, Peter also denied knowing Jesus three times when he found himself in a position where it might cost him something to associate with Jesus.

Mary Magdalene wasn't perfect. She was a woman with a reputation.

Martha wasn't perfect, even though she wanted to be; she was a perfectionist who would rather work for Jesus than spend time with Him.

David, Peter, Mary, Martha, and the list goes on—not one of them was perfect. They were all flawed, yet God chose to love them just as He chooses to love you in spite of your flaws. God chose to use each of these people for His glory. The secret to

God's working powerfully through you is not your abilities, but God's. It is His power working through you that makes all the difference. You simply have to say yes to His call and daily seek to walk with Him, not looking to the right or the left, but keeping your eyes focused on Him. He will lead you. He will guide you.

This is the message of the gospel; it is the good news everyone talks about. Regardless of your flaws, faults, mistakes, and mishaps, God still loves you. That is what I want to encourage you with today. Don't be disappointed in yourself. Just as children make mistakes as they are growing and turning into adults, so do young Christians as they grow into mature Christians. God's love for you, His daughter, does not depend on your perfection or achievements. Rather it depends on your acceptance of His grace. It depends on what Jesus did on that bloody, brutal cross over two thousand years ago. Your price has already been paid by the One who lovingly chose to lay His life down for yours. Release the heavy burden of perfection and live in the love and grace Jesus freely offers to you (Matthew 11:30).

One of my favorite truths about Christ is found in Hebrews 4:15–16 (NIV):

> *We do not have a high priest who is unable to sympathize*
> *with our weaknesses, but we have one who has been tempted*
> *in every way, just as we are—yet he did not sin. Let us*
> *then approach God's throne of grace with confidence, so*
> *that we may receive mercy and find grace to help us in*
> *our time of need.*

Why is this one of my favorite verses? It clearly states that Jesus understands our weaknesses. He is on a throne of grace; He is the giver of mercy and grace, helping us in our times of need.

Jesus paid the price to release us from the bondage of living a perfect life. He doesn't want sacrifice; He wants a relationship— a relationship built on trust in Him and in His promises. He wants our hearts, our love, our devotion, and, yes, our obedience. But He wants our obedience to flow out of our love for Him and our desire to bring Him glory through our lives, not out of our need to look or be perfect.

As I'm growing in the Lord, I'm learning to embrace my thorn. Oh, don't get me wrong—I still would love to wish it away many days, but now I'm realizing that this thorn in my flesh is actually a way for me to give all the glory to God. And for that I am thankful. Anything good that comes from my life is a result of the good He has done in and through me. I am merely the fragile clay in the Potter's hand.

Mold me into Your image every day, sweet Jesus. May I look more and more like You and less and less like me. I am abandoning perfection and embracing hope-filled grace. Join me?

Reflection Questions

1. How has God used "thorns" in your life to help carve you into
   His image?

2. To what lies concerning God's love for you are you currently
   listening? Take some time now to read Romans 5:8 and
   Ephesians 3:17-19. Pray and ask God to help you understand
   the love He has for you and for your eyes and mind to be
   opened to His truth and presence in your life.

3. *Looking at Matthew 11:28-29, what are some burdens you
    have been carrying that Christ never meant for you to carry?
    Make a list and then pray through the list, crossing each one
    off after you've prayed and given that burden over to God.*

4. *After reading Hebrews 4:15-16, consider: How does God's
    Word help you approach Him with confidence instead of fear?
    What does that tell you about God's expectations of you?*

Prayer:

*Dear Jesus, thank You for Your love. Thank You for loving us enough
to go to the cross and die in our place. Thank You for the unique ways
You have made each of us. Please open our eyes and minds to better
understand how high, wide, and deep the love You have for us truly is.
On the days that we doubt Your love, remind us to run to the Scriptures
instead of to the world to find it. Help us to understand Your love so
that we can better love those You have placed in our lives. May we be a
light in this dark world, showing Your glory for all to see. Amen.*

Week 4: Monday

Read: Romans 5:6-11

SOAP: Romans 5:6, 8

S Write out the **Scripture** passage for the day.

O Write down one or two **observations** from the passage.

A Write down one or two **applications** from the passage.

P **Pray** over what you learned from today's passage.

Week 4: Tuesday

Read: Ephesians 2:1-5

SOAP: Ephesians 2:4

S   Write out the **Scripture** passage for the day.

O   Write down one or two **observations** from the passage.

A   Write down one or two **applications** from the passage.

P   **Pray** over what you learned from today's passage.

Week 4: Wednesday

Read: Ephesians 2:6-10

SOAP: Ephesians 2:8-9

S Write out the **Scripture** passage for the day.

O Write down one or two **observations** from the passage.

A Write down one or two **applications** from the passage.

P **Pray** over what you learned from today's passage.

Week 4: Thursday

Read: 1 John 4:10-12

SOAP: 1 John 4:10-12

S　Write out the **Scripture** passage for the day.

O　Write down one or two **observations** from the passage.

A　Write down one or two **applications** from the passage.

P　**Pray** over what you learned from today's passage.

Week 4: Friday

Read: Hebrews 4:15–16

SOAP: Hebrews 4:15–16

S Write out the **Scripture** passage for the day.

O Write down one or two **observations** from the passage.

A Write down one or two **applications** from the passage.

P **Pray** over what you learned from today's passage.

Week 5

Week 5 Challenge:

Let me encourage you to start a trust journal and begin recording all the ways God has been trustworthy in your life. Many times in my own life I, regrettably, have not been faithful in remembering all the ways God has been faithful to me, even though at the time I swore I would never forget. Taking time to look back and remember builds upon the evidence that God is indeed trustworthy. He always has been, and He always will be.

May I offer a few journal prompts to get you started:

· My earliest memory of God being near me was . . .

· Identify a time when you really had to trust God and recall how God worked in that situation.

- Record some of your favorite verses that talk about trusting God. How do those verses give you hope during the hard seasons in your life?

- How can you step out in faith and trust God more with your life? What are some action steps that you can take today?

Week 5 Memory Verse

Trust in the LORD with all your heart

and lean not on your own understanding;

in all your ways submit to him,

and he will make your paths straight.

Proverbs 3:5-6, NIV

CHAPTER 5

You Can Trust Him

Angela

GOD SEES YOU. He made you, knows you, and loves you. You can trust Him. Part of our issue with not fully surrendering our lives to Jesus is that we don't really know if we can trust Him.

Joseph learned how to trust God when his brothers sold him into slavery (see Genesis 37, 39–41). Rahab had to learn to trust God for who He is, rather than what she was (see Joshua 2). We see in Rahab's story that when we place our faith in who God is, He does what He says He will do. God keeps His promises.

You can trust Him.

Remember, dear friend, God sees the big picture.

When you realize your life is held in His loving hands, you can begin to release it to the One who breathed life into you (Genesis 2:7). Take confidence, not in your own abilities, but in His. Trust in His work in your life (Philippians 2:13).

We live in a broken world where people have failed us. Dads, who were supposed to help us understand God's love for His children, have left us, abused us, or failed us in other ways. No wonder so many of us struggle with trusting God, because we have not been able to trust the fathers in our lives. But we must remember we live in a broken world. God does not necessarily operate the way your dad did. God is completely holy, completely loving, and completely trustworthy.

Your life is in God's hands (John 10:28-29), and nothing can touch you that does not first go through Him (John 19:11). I know that can be a hard truth to swallow, especially if you have been hurt or abused in the past. Questions such as *How can a loving God allow this to happen to me*? fill your mind in the middle of the night. Here's my take on the issue. God sees the whole picture where I see only my life and my limited view of it. I know from Scripture that He works all things out for those who love Him and are called according to His purposes (Romans 8:28). I have to trust that even in the hard and tough times in my life, God can and will bring something beautiful out of it. We simply have to trust Him in this, even when we don't yet see the fruits of it in our lives.

Through the pain of being labeled learning disabled, I had to learn that He would eventually use it for good. It was hard. I was hurt, and at times I am still healing. But God is good (Psalm 136:1), and I trust Him to use all things in our lives to bring us closer to Him and also to bring Him glory.

That is the true purpose of our lives—to bring God glory (Matthew 5:16). This life is not about me, and it is not about you either. It is all about God and telling others about Him through the lives we have been blessed to live.

I was in my Sunday school class a few weeks ago, and we were talking about the importance of bringing God glory. I can see why God's desire to be glorified might sound rather self-ish to someone who does not have a personal relationship with

Him. I sat there listening to what everyone was sharing, but my heart started racing, and I felt I needed to share one small nugget of truth with them. Yes, the purpose of our lives is to glorify God. Plain and simple. When we know that truth, our lives can become much easier and simpler. Hard life questions can become easier when we hold everything up against that truth. Here's the thing: Our lives are all about giving God glory, but not because He needs it. Even the rocks can call out His name (Luke 19:40). When He is glorified through our lives, He uses that to bring more lives to Himself. It is not selfish. It is the most loving thing He can do. It all comes back to God loving us.

Can you trust God? Yes.

Is it hard? Yes.

Is it worth it? Yes!

Over the years I have learned to view my life through a few different lenses. The first one is that God is love (1 John 4:8). Even when I don't understand what is happening in the world— why evil is allowed to prevail at times, why children are hurt or murdered—I come back to this truth: God is love. He sees it all. It doesn't mean He condones it. It doesn't mean He planned it that way, but He sees it all, and He can and will bring good out of it, in His time, in His own way. He is the great El Roi, the One who sees and the One who restores (Psalm 80:3).

Right after my third grade year, my parents divorced. Although I told a friend during summer school that I would be moving soon, I had no idea what was in store. My fourth grade year was difficult. I was at a new school with different kids, in an unfamiliar house, and in a strange town. My mom was now a single parent. She worked as a hairdresser during the day and went back to school in the evening to try and make life better for my brother and me.

We moved into a small two-bedroom duplex. We couldn't take showers or baths at that place because when we turned the water on, dead ants and orange-colored, rusty water flowed from the pipes. Besides, the smell of the water was so bad I vividly remember holding my breath and trying to brush my teeth fast enough so that I wouldn't have to smell it.

As a child, times were tough. One evening at the local grocery store, a man started flirting with my mom when he noticed she wasn't wearing a wedding ring. He began following us around the store, and when my mom didn't respond to his advances, he became angry. He started saying all kinds of degrading things to her, and I remember being scared and angry with him at the same time. In my innocence I wanted to protect my mom but didn't know how. After aisles and aisles of the man following us around the store, he finally left after he started getting some looks from fellow shoppers.

Not having a father figure in the family can make you feel vulnerable. It's not as if my father was around a lot when I was growing up. He wasn't. Partly it was due to his job and partly because he chose to travel, but either way my mom, brother, and I were accustomed to being alone. After the divorce, that sense of the three of us being alone felt different. It was almost as if our sense of security had been taken away, and I felt vulnerable.

Being a single parent is rough. Being the child of a single parent is hard too. But through that hard time in my life, God was right there in the midst of us, even when I didn't feel Him. I'm learning that in my life. He is always there, even when I can't feel Him, even when it feels as though He's not listening to my prayers, even when my prayers go unanswered. He is still next to me, loving me, looking over me, and carrying me through the painful days. Oftentimes I didn't see His hand at work in my life until the situation was over and I was able to look back on it. That's when I could see His fingerprints all over the situation and how He had been faithful in orchestrating the events and working on my behalf.

It's no different in this story. As my family was going through this incredibly hard time, Jesus had placed us right where we were supposed to live, across the street from Stephanie, Whitney, and their family. Through the pain, God supplied friends who would help us, walk beside us, and travel with us through life. Whitney's and Stephanie's mom had walked a similar path just a few years prior to my family moving across the street. Their mom comforted my mom as they let us use their washing machine to wash our clothes. Though we lived there for only a year, that's all that was needed. God used that hard year to knit our hearts together and begin a friendship that would span twenty-plus years.

Stephanie and Whitney's mom loved on my mom, offered advice, listened, and best of all just did life with her. It's so nice to have a friend who chooses to walk beside you through your pain. It's even nicer to have a friend who chooses to walk beside you because she understands the path on which you are walking. She knows the fears, the pain, and the need to have someone with you to comfort you and remind you that you're not alone.

That year God began something beautiful in all of our lives. He brought beauty out of our ashes (Isaiah 61:3). He birthed love and friendship out of pain (Psalm 34:18).

Though Stephanie and I were neighbors for only a year, she and I remain friends to this day. Instead of next-door neighbors, we became pen pals. Or I should say she became a pen pal. She was the writer, and I was the reader. (How in the world did I ever become a blogger? Only by the grace of God!) As we were growing up, Stephanie and I would see each other about once a year, normally when I would travel back to Indiana to visit my grandparents. Over the years we attended each other's high school graduation parties, were in each other's weddings, and visited one another for the births of our children. I have three girls, and she has three boys. If we believed in prearranged marriages, our children would be all set!

Over the years I also had opportunities to stay in contact with Whitney, Stephanie's older sister. Whitney and I would see each other when I would be invited to join in a family gathering. Stephanie kept me updated on what Whitney and her family were doing through the years. Then one night a few years ago, I ran across a blog post Whitney had written and shared on Facebook. I clicked on the link and read the post and loved what she said and how she said it. I felt that I was sitting in her family room, snuggled up with a warm cup of tea, talking with a dear friend.

I sent her a message over Facebook, telling her how much her post had encouraged me. Soon we were corresponding regularly about our blogs. Over the course of a few weeks, Whitney and I talked, prayed, and sought the Lord, and finally one morning I woke up to find an e-mail in my in-box in which Whitney told me she would be honored to serve alongside me in my online community, Love God Greatly. What God had started years ago when I was a little girl, through pain and heartache, He was now redeeming. He was bringing purpose and beauty out of it. God allowed the hurt because He saw a greater good emerging from the ashes of broken homes and broken dreams.

I have learned to trust God because I have seen Him work in

my life. Looking back, I am now thankful for the hard times and difficulties God allowed me to walk through in my younger years because I have learned to rely only on Him. At times He is all I had. Many times in our lives, the hard days are the times when we are refined to look and love more like Jesus. The hard days chip away at our rough edges, our pride, and our independent ways. I am grateful now that God has not rescued me from all my pain, disappointments, and sadness, because it has been through those experiences that I have been able to grow stronger in my faith. The longer I live, the more opportunities I have to learn to trust God based on my past experiences with Him. With each opportunity my life becomes a living testimony, a way to give glory to God and help encourage those who are in tough seasons of their lives to trust Him.

Remember, sweet sister, you can trust Him.

Reflection Questions

1. *Take a few minutes to look back on your own life. How has God been faithful to you in the past?*

2. *Think back on a time when you felt someone failed you. What do you think God's purpose was for that hurtful situation? What good came out of it?*

3. How does realizing that nothing can touch you that doesn't first come through God help you trust Him more?

4. What are some of the "lenses" through which you view your life?

5. Who has God placed in your life to help you through the hard paths you have had to walk? Consider writing that person a letter and thanking him or her for how God used him or her in your life.

Prayer:

Dear Jesus, thank You for how You go before us and behind us. Thank You for Your unending love—a love that is not based on what we can do but rather on what You have already done. Thank You for how You lovingly place challenges in our lives where we have to look to You, learning to trust You as we learn to walk with You through our lives. Please continue to grow us into Your image; help us to glorify You with the lives You've blessed us with. We are Yours, so move mightily through us and help us to be Your hands and feet to a hurting world that desperately needs to know they can trust You. Amen.

Week 5: Monday

Read: Psalm 84

SOAP: Psalm 84:11-12

S   Write out the **Scripture** passage for the day.

O   Write down one or two **observations** from the passage.

A   Write down one or two **applications** from the passage.

P   **Pray** over what you learned from today's passage.

Week 5: Tuesday

Read: Proverbs 3:5-6

SOAP: Proverbs 3:5-6

S Write out the **Scripture** passage for the day.

O Write down one or two **observations** from the passage.

A Write down one or two **applications** from the passage.

P Pray over what you learned from today's passage.

Week 5: Wednesday

Read: Psalm 9:7–10

SOAP: Psalm 9:10

S Write out the **Scripture** passage for the day.

O Write down one or two **observations** from the passage.

A Write down one or two **applications** from the passage.

P **Pray** over what you learned from today's passage.

Week 5: Thursday

Read: Romans 8:28-30

SOAP: Romans 8:28, 30

S   Write out the **Scripture** passage for the day.

O   Write down one or two **observations** from the passage.

A   Write down one or two **applications** from the passage.

P   **Pray** over what you learned from today's passage.

Week 5: Friday

Read: John 10:27-30

SOAP: John 10:28-29

S   Write out the **Scripture** passage for the day.

O   Write down one or two **observations** from the passage.

A   Write down one or two **applications** from the passage.

P   **Pray** over what you learned from today's passage.

Week 6

Week 6 Challenge:

Write down three names of friends or family members who do not have a personal relationship with Jesus yet. Ask God to give you opportunities to share about the difference Christ makes in your life. If God opens the door, invite them to church or to an event where they will hear about the love of Christ for them. Love them where they are, but pray for God to move in their hearts to want to know Him. I'll be joining you and covering you in prayer, praying for opportunities and for courage. Praying for you, sweet friend, that you will be a loving, shining light for our Lord in the community where Jesus has placed you.

Week 6 Memory Verse:

If we are children, then we are heirs—heirs of God and co-heirs with Christ, if indeed we share in his sufferings in order that we may also share in his glory.

Romans 8:17, NIV

CHAPTER 6

You're Invited

Angela

I LOVE THE STORY OF Moses because I feel I can personally relate to him so well. He was a man called by God to lead his people to freedom, yet he didn't feel he was the right one for the job. He felt inadequate and thought, *Surely God made a mistake on this assignment. I'm not the right guy.* Moses was even brave enough to tell God this:

> *"Pardon your servant, Lord. I have never been eloquent, neither in the past nor since you have spoken to your servant. I am slow of speech and tongue."*
>
> *The LORD said to him, "Who gave human beings their mouths? Who makes them deaf or mute? Who gives them sight or makes them blind? Is it not I, the LORD? Now go; I will help you speak and will teach you what to say."*
>
> *But Moses said, "Pardon your servant, Lord. Please send someone else."*
> EXODUS 4:10–13, NIV

Moses felt so unqualified for the job God called him to do. Moses thought he had to be somebody before God could use him.

I don't know about you, but I've found myself having those very same thoughts. But you know what? We have it all backward. Because of our relationship with Jesus, we already are somebody, a treasured and loved daughter of the King of kings (Romans 8:16-17), and Jesus has already equipped us for the task He is calling us to do (Hebrews 13:21). We just need to live in obedience to His call on our lives and trust Him every step of the way.

So many Christians these days feel they have to do huge things for God in order to make a real impact on our world. I beg to differ; God can use you mightily for His Kingdom right where you are, with the people He has already placed in your life.

In the 1960s there were two little girls who were friends at school. One little girl named Peggy knew about God because she came from a home where both Mom and Dad tucked her into bed at night and gave her kisses after her prayers. The other little girl named Diana did not know God because she came from a home where Daddy had left and only her mommy tucked her into bed at night with kisses but no prayers.

Peggy's mom had a personal relationship with Jesus. Peggy saw her mom open her Bible in the mornings to read it and spend some sweet time with Jesus. Peggy's mom talked to her about God, about the importance of telling others about God's love and free gift of salvation. Peggy's mom made Jesus' mission in life of seeking and saving the lost her mission in life, too, so she passed that same desire and passion on to her daughter.

One day Peggy asked Diana if she would like to go to church with her and her family. Diana agreed, and after begging her mom, Diana was finally allowed to go. That night at Peggy's little country church, there was an altar call. Diana was too afraid to walk down the long aisle past all the people to the unknown pastor down front, so she decided to stay in her seat and ask Jesus into her heart right where she was sitting. Neither Peggy nor her parents were aware that Diana asked Jesus to come into her heart that night. Diana kept it just between God and her. From Peggy and her parents' perspective, God didn't do anything that night in that poor child's life.

Peggy's mom knew the importance of being in God's Word, spending time in prayer, and being sensitive to simple requests, such as, "Mom, can we bring Diana to church with us tonight?" Because of her own walk with God, Peggy's mom influenced her daughter to be mission minded and to reach out to those who might not be 100 percent like her, those who came from broken homes or who had broken hearts, to extend the invitation and put the result in God's hands.

The story you have just read is my story because one of those little girls, Diana, is my mom. God began my family's spiritual legacy with a simple invitation. Peggy and her mom had no idea what God was starting through them when they took Diana to church one Sunday night. To them nothing had happened. They did not see the change that had taken place in Diana's heart. They did not witness the fact that God had used them to steer a whole family, who was once far from God, to Him, and all through a simple invitation from a child.

God uses ordinary women and children and does extraordinary things through their lives, through their simple acts of obedience. An invitation was extended and accepted because of a mom who walked with God and taught her daughter the importance of sharing God's free gift of salvation. Thousands of women around the world are now encouraged to be in God's Word and to love Him greatly with their lives.

God is always at work. Sometimes we are blessed to see what He is doing through us; sometimes the blessing is waiting for us when we get to heaven, but nevertheless, God is always at work.

As sisters, daughters, mothers, and friends, we all play a part in God's amazing redemption plan. He has a beautiful purpose for each of our lives. I love how God used a mom and her daughter to bring my family to Christ. He chose them first! Do you see that? He chose those who possibly felt insignificant to begin the mighty work. Yes, I'm so thankful to men and women like Billy Graham and Beth Moore who have inspired and taught my mom through the years, but God didn't choose them to plant the seed of faith. He chose an ordinary mom and her daughter in rural Indiana, far from the limelight, who went to a simple country church with no dynamic speakers or worship leaders, just the regular folks from their town. Folks like you and me. God saw them and chose them. He still does the same today.

We read in Jeremiah 29:11 that God has a plan and purpose for our lives. We are the body of Christ, and God has gifted each of us uniquely for His beautiful plan. No one's role is more important than anyone else's. We were made to touch the future with our lives through our walk with God in the here and now, in the seemingly insignificant and mundane days of our lives.

Our main job here on earth is to give Him glory as moms, grandmas, working women, and single women. Every stage and area of our lives should point to Jesus. We were made to live lives larger than ourselves, and we need to make every day count. You never know who is watching and whose life might be impacted by a simple gesture like Peggy's.

Be encouraged today, because God loves doing big things through women and children. Don't believe me? Just look at what He did through Mary and Jesus, or what about that crazy story in John where we find Jesus feeding five thousand people from a simple lunch of bread and fish? Who had enough faith to give Jesus all that he had? A little boy. And who do you think made that lunch for him? Now, I'm not a betting woman, but if I were, I'd put my money on his mom.

Are you starting to see how time and time again God shows us through the Bible how He uses ordinary moms and children to change the world? Those who feel weak He makes strong (2 Corinthians 12:9).

Don't for a second place a value on your life by what you see. What you are doing in your home with your kids, in your neighborhood, and in your community matters. Your walk with our Lord is important. How you choose to invest your life matters. Be a woman who plants simple seeds of faith in your home, workplace, and schools. Then trust God to water those seeds and create a mighty harvest.

Don't think for a second that God can't use you mightily for His Kingdom right in the midst of raising kids and taking their friends to church. Sometimes, many times, it's in the everyday tasks that God is working. Yes, there are miracles in the mundane.

Be a woman who lives your life on purpose—a woman who carries Jesus' mission in your heart and passes that same mission on to your children. Like Peggy's mom, play the part He created you to play. You may not see how a simple yes to a simple invitation can change the world, but God does.

Let's choose together to be women who love God greatly with our lives, planting simple seeds of faith throughout our lives as we walk with our King. We are in this together. Play your part, know God has a beautiful purpose for your life, and remember that one day you will meet Jesus face-to-face. Focus your life on that moment.

Just as the invitation was extended to my mom so many years ago, God also reaches out His hands and extends the same invitation to you. You're invited, sweet friend. Play your part. Join the team. It won't be the same without you.

Reflection Questions

1. *Who can you be a "Peggy's mom" to in your life? Pray and write down some ways you can intentionally introduce them to God.*

2. *In what ways can you be obedient to God right now in the mundane tasks of your life? Ask God to open your eyes and help you see the greater purpose He is working in and through you.*

3. *How did your spiritual legacy begin? Write it down and take time to thank God for how He is working in and through your family.*

4. *What are some ways God is calling you to be a light for Him in your community?*

5. *Remember, you don't have to come from a perfect family for God to do something perfectly wonderful through you. Read about King Josiah in 2 Kings 21:19–23:29 and discuss his lineage in light of this idea.*

Prayer:

Dear Jesus, thank You for including us in Your amazing story of redemption. What a privilege it is to serve You and be used by You. Please Lord, help us to be women who reach out to the hurting world and share Your gift of salvation. Help us to be in the world, but not of the world. Thank You for the communities in which You have placed each of us, and help us to have a passion for those who don't know You. Give us the love that we need to reach these hurting sisters and brothers. Strengthen us, Lord, through Your Word and through each other. Unite us around You and our love for You. Bless our efforts, and open hearts and minds to Your truth. Amen.

Week 6: Monday

Read: Romans 8:14-17

SOAP: Romans 8:16-17

S Write out the **Scripture** passage for the day.

O Write down one or two **observations** from the passage.

A Write down one or two **applications** from the passage.

P **Pray** over what you learned from today's passage.

Week 6: Tuesday

Read: Hebrews 13:20-21

SOAP: Hebrews 13:21

S   Write out the **Scripture** passage for the day.

O   Write down one or two **observations** from the passage.

A   Write down one or two **applications** from the passage.

P   **Pray** over what you learned from today's passage.

Week 6: Wednesday

Read: Jeremiah 29:11-13

SOAP: Jeremiah 29:11

S Write out the **Scripture** passage for the day.

O Write down one or two **observations** from the passage.

A Write down one or two **applications** from the passage.

P **Pray** over what you learned from today's passage.

Week 6: Thursday

Read: 2 Corinthians 12:9-10

SOAP: 2 Corinthians 12:9

S   Write out the **Scripture** passage for the day.

O   Write down one or two **observations** from the passage.

A   Write down one or two **applications** from the passage.

P   **Pray** over what you learned from today's passage.

Week 6: Friday

Read: Revelation 19:6–9

SOAP: Revelation 19:9

S Write out the **Scripture** passage for the day.

O Write down one or two **observations** from the passage.

A Write down one or two **applications** from the passage.

P Pray over what you learned from today's passage.

Week 7

Week 7 Challenge:

Loving others seems so very easy as an idea, but it is hard to apply in real life. When you love generously and affirm the worth of others you meet, you are acting like Jesus Himself. If you are to mature in your life, you must practice initiating love in your heart and in reality to those who might be difficult to love. Also, there may be non-Christians in your life who need to see your love before they will ever believe in the love of God.

List below anyone in your life—neighbor, friend, coworker, child, family member, or spouse—who needs to know or feel the love of God in his or her life.

Plan one thing you will do to show them His love. Try to list at least two people to whom you will seek to show the love of God. (Write a note or e-mail, meet them for coffee, make them a meal, take them a flower, call them on the phone, spend time with them.)

Week 7 Memory Verse:

A new command I give you: Love one another. As I have loved you, so you must love one another. By this everyone will know that you are my disciples, if you love one another.

John 13:34–35, NIV

CHAPTER 7

Loving Is Our Kingdom Work

Beloved, if God so loved us, we also ought to love one another.

1 JOHN 4:11

Tears welling up in her large brown eyes, my friend looked down as I approached her and said, "If you really knew me, you would not want to be my friend."

Attending a secular leadership conference by myself with over eight hundred people had made me quite shy. Yet the first night I attended this conference in a large hotel ballroom, a sweet woman called out to me, "I have an empty seat next to me. Do you want to join me?"

And so we began talking, and from that night on, we sat together. Over the course of the four days, we had talked and shared some of our life stories with one another and we were becoming real pals.

That is how one of my sweetest friendships began. My new friend took the time to initiate a conversation with me. She actually showed interest in my life, which opened my heart.

One morning I said to her, "Tell me all about yourself! I would love to know your life story!"

How surprised I was to see her tears begin flowing and hear her pronouncement that I would not like her if I really knew her. I had been delighted to have her friendship in a crowd of strangers.

"There is something I have not told you," she whispered, "and when you know, you will be ashamed of me, and ashamed to be my friend.

"I have been married and divorced three times, and I didn't want you to know."

I took her lovely face into my hands and said, "You have befriended me. You bubble over when you talk. You reach out to everyone you know. You are interesting, intelligent, attractive, loving, and that is what I know about you, my sweet friend. I would never define you by your past. I love who you are right now, just as you are, and I am so very thankful for you!"

Her eyes widened as though she couldn't believe what I was saying. We gave each other a warm embrace. She said, "No one has ever loved me like that before. Even my mother had a hard time accepting my loud, extroverted personality and I have been looking for love my whole life. That is why I kept leaving my marriages; because they didn't fill my need for love."

And then, during the last day of the conference, she opened her heart to the love of Jesus. She needed to feel the love of a friend whom she could see before she could believe in the love of God that she had to imagine. And so I left her a candle and card at the front desk as a visible evidence of love.

I received a text from her at the airport and read, "No one has ever shown me this kind of generous love in my whole life. I feel like a new person. You have changed my life forever."

Love is God's universal language, which reaches into the hearts of others and shows them their worth in God's eyes and in ours! Loving others is the basis for our Kingdom work—spreading the Kingdom of Jesus in our world by sowing the seeds of Jesus' love. Often people cannot even begin to understand the love and forgiveness of God's love until they have felt real love from a real person.

Why must we initiate love before others love us? Because that is what Jesus did. "We love, because He first loved us." (1 John 4:19). God's love was initiated to us before we even knew to ask Him to help us.

We read in Romans that while we were yet sinners—when we weren't even thinking about Him—Christ died for us because He saw our need.

Jesus modeled His love for the world by showing love to prostitutes, tax collectors, children, Roman soldiers, lepers, and common folk like fishermen and friends—His demeanor was to seek and save the lost, lonely, and all who needed to know His love gently flowing into their own needy hearts.

Love is a choice for us to extend His love to others.

Even as Christ is the One who pursues us, provides for us, encourages us, comforts us, and speaks love over us, so we must understand that we are to pursue others in life-giving love. Because He is the source, the beginning and definition of generous, unconditional love, and because He lives within us, we must be a picture of His initiating love to all who come into our lives.

We are His hands to bless others.

We are His voice to give messages of love to those who need to hear these messages.

We are His servants, living in such a way that others can see God through us.

Love is an obedient choice. When you choose to love others, that is the moment you are most like Jesus.

Love heals relationships.

Love is a salve to wounds.

Love is the beginning of friendship.

Love initiates.

Love inspires others.

Love comforts.

Love says, "You are worth knowing and I want to be friends with you."

Peter says in 1 Peter 4:8, "Above all, keep fervent in your love for one another, because love covers a multitude of sins."

Even as my friend allowed her feelings of failure and her shame to be a reason to draw back from me, so often the failures or immaturity of our own lives keep us from loving well.

I have learned that growing in our ability to show and give God's love is a process. Sometimes showing love to others is awkward, and we have to be patient to give it without expecting something in return.

The Process of Love

Loving well may take time. Learning to speak love into the lives of others is a discipline that grows with practice. The more I seek to give love, regardless of someone else's response, the easier it is.

Being patient and forgiving of those who hurt us is also a practice that grows in our hearts with time. We start out taking baby steps and grow stronger each time we practice it. And we find that as Jesus humbles us and shows us our own selfishness, we are more apt to be forgiving of others.

The older I become, the more mistakes I have made, and the

more humbled I have become. The forgiveness and love of Jesus mean even more to me now because I see myself as I really am—and still He loves and forgives me. That amazes me and makes me much more humble and forgiving to others. It has been a process of growth over my whole life.

False pride or a critical attitude that tells someone else "I am better than you!" can be a detriment to our ability to love others. Jesus said, "He who is without sin, cast the first stone," when the Pharisees brought a prostitute before Him to condemn her (see John 8:7). Yet Jesus was saying, "When you look at your own heart and find that there is not sin there, then you can judge someone else."

Criticizing others because we think we are better than them grieves the heart of Jesus and quenches His Spirit's love through us.

In one of His parables, Jesus spoke well of a man who beat his breast and said, "Oh Lord, I am a sinner. How can You forgive me?" And He insinuated that because the man saw His need for God, He came to redemption. Yet the Pharisee who patted himself on the back for being righteous was not commended for his faith—his pride separated him from God and from others whom Jesus would want to have redeemed (see Luke 18).

Another reason it is often difficult to love others is that we have been hurt deeply by them. Often, we pull away from people because they have hurt us or been unfair, judged us, or gossiped about us. Yet holding a grudge or choosing to be bitter toward others only injures our own souls. If we wrap ourselves in the cloak of selfishness, condemnation of others, grudges, and unforgiveness, we will always be sad and disappointed in others. Often I have heard a woman say, "No one ever talks to me" or "No one ever initiates a conversation with me."

This kind of attitude will never produce fruit. Because most of the people we come into contact with do not know the love of Jesus, it is probable that we, like Jesus, will be called to give far more than we receive. We cannot expect those who are not mature or redeemed to exhibit God's love to us.

But if we have experienced the love and grace of God, then we are the ones responsible to be the givers and peacemakers. Only love and forgiveness can heal us and heal others so that they can come to Christ.

Sometimes those we choose to love cannot love us back and continue in the habits of criticism, harshness, or passivity. Yet even though we cannot control the behavior of others, we are still called to love. Whether or not someone responds to our love is not our responsibility—we are to be obedient and leave the results in God's hands.

The more we practice love, the more we end up loving Jesus. The more we realize how much it cost Him to give His love to undeserving, ungrateful people, the more we will worship Him, the Perfect One, for being willing to lay down His life for us!

The way we live daily, seeking to grow in showing our love to others, becomes a legacy of His love in the lives of others. We are the gospel message many will read. Our acts of kindness and thoughtfulness will open hearts to His love because others will imagine a God who is good because they have seen His goodness expressed toward them.

Reflection Questions

1. *The way we love others is a mark of our belonging to Christ. According to the verse below, what does it mean to you, in practical ways, to show Jesus' love every day in your life?*

    To your friends? Your children? Your husband? Your coworkers? Your neighbors?

By this all men will know that you are My disciples,
   if you have love for one another.

JOHN 13:35

2. *What are the ways people communicate love to you? When do you feel most loved by others?*

3. *Examine your heart and try to see if there is someone toward whom you are harboring resentment. Write about this situation in your journal and ask God to show you how to love that person.*

4. *John 15:13 says, "Greater love has no one than this, that one lay down his life for his friends." What areas do you need to "lay down," or put aside, in order to show the servant love of Jesus to others?*

5. *"I am convinced that neither death, nor life, nor angels, nor principalities, nor things present, nor things to come, nor powers, nor height, nor depth, nor any other created thing, will be able to separate us from the love of God, which is in Christ Jesus our Lord" (Romans 8:38-39).*

    According to this verse, there is no circumstance, no problem, no failure that can ever separate us from the love of God. In what ways do people need to see this kind of love that will never change, never grow cold, never condemn?

6. *Make a plan with three action items for how you are determined to grow stronger in showing God's love through your life.*

Prayer:

Dear Heavenly Father, please help us to see the eyes of everyone in our lives from Your point of view. Help us to more deeply understand that it is Your unconditional love that transforms and reaches hearts. For all of those who are broken, wounded, and separated from Your love, help us to love in such a way that we bring healing, comfort, understanding, and grace to those who long deeply to be loved. May all who see us feel that they have seen the very love of God because of the ways we love them. We come in Jesus' name, amen.

Week 7: Monday

Read: 1 John 4:16–21

SOAP: 1 John 4:19–21

S Write out the **Scripture** passage for the day.

O Write down one or two **observations** from the passage.

A Write down one or two **applications** from the passage.

P **Pray** over what you learned from today's passage.

Week 7: Tuesday

Read: 1 Peter 4:8-11

SOAP: 1 Peter 4:8

S Write out the **Scripture** passage for the day.

O Write down one or two **observations** from the passage.

A Write down one or two **applications** from the passage.

P **Pray** over what you learned from today's passage.

Week 7: Wednesday

Read: John 13:34–35

SOAP: John 13:34–35

S   Write out the **Scripture** passage for the day.

O   Write down one or two **observations** from the passage.

A   Write down one or two **applications** from the passage.

P   **Pray** over what you learned from today's passage.

Week 7: Thursday

Read: John 15:9-17

SOAP: John 15:12-13

S   Write out the **Scripture** passage for the day.

O   Write down one or two **observations** from the passage.

A   Write down one or two **applications** from the passage.

P   **Pray** over what you learned from today's passage.

Week 7: Friday

Read: 1 John 3:16-24

SOAP: 1 John 3:23-24

S Write out the **Scripture** passage for the day.

O Write down one or two **observations** from the passage.

A Write down one or two **applications** from the passage.

P **Pray** over what you learned from today's passage.

Week 8

Week 8 Challenge:

God showed His love for us in that while we were sinners, He took the initiative to come to the world to die for us. Love initiates without being asked. As you leave the fragrance of God throughout your life by initiating love, showing kindness, and giving your time and focus to those who come across your life, you will stand out. We live in a very isolated world where so few people take the initiative or time to care for others.

As a final application of this book, write down two habits in your life you would like to practice that will help you not only respond to people when they need you but also push you to initiate God's love to them. It might be as easy as "I will make it a habit to ask questions of new people whom God brings into my life." ("Hi, I noticed you are new. Tell me about yourself. What brings you to our town?") Or you might determine to think of two people whom you might invite to join you for Bible study. Can you think of two practices that you would like to adopt that will help you take the initiative in reaching out to others whom God providentially brings your way?

Week 8 Memory Verse:

Jesus replied: "'Love the Lord your God with all your heart and with all your soul and with all your mind.' This is the first and greatest commandment."

Matthew 22:37-38, NIV

CHAPTER 8

Love as a Way of Life

Sally

Greater love has no one than this: to lay down one's life for one's friends.

JESUS, IN JOHN 15:13, NIV

New York City is awhirl with opportunities: the lights of Broadway, international cafés, and the excitement of business and trade. It is filled with international communities, acting schools, and so many other inviting lures. It is also a place of ghettos, drug dealers, bars, and a host of temptations. Yet this is where my nineteen-year-old son, Nathan, had received a scholarship to attend New York Film Academy.

As a mother, I hoped I had trained him to make good decisions, to walk with God in the midst of temptation, to be safe from the dangers of a big city; yet I knew at my core that I had no control over my son's life. I would have to leave him in God's hands.

Early one morning, after he had been bedazzled by the city, Nathan was jogging in a park near his apartment. As he ran, he said it was as though God spoke to him:

What kind of story are you going to write with your life? You are the one who will determine your reputation. People are only victims if they let their circumstances determine how they behave.

There are so many ways your life can go now that you are on your own in a big city with lots of pathways—those that could destroy your life and those that will create a life of godliness. Which life will you pursue? Will you chase after the world, or will you chase after Me?

My son said that at that point, he realized he would have to decide to chase after God and His ways if he wanted to grow in godliness and write a great story with his life. He knew his life would not be great if he did not, by an act of his will, make the choices every day to stay pure, to make moral choices, to read God's Word, and to act in love.

As Nathan got to know people in his class, he realized that he was one of the only believers out of over one hundred people. He made it his goal to reach out to those different from himself, to befriend a group of men he could encourage, and to live a life of integrity so that all who knew him would want to know his Lord Jesus.

A graduation celebration took place at the end of his final semester. After the ceremony, there was a party with all of his classmates that, of course, included a lot of drinking and celebrating. Yet Nathan went to the party to be with the very friends he had been praying for all year. He did not drink with them, but he determined to tell each person how glad he was to have met him or her, as he wanted to leave one last impression of God's love.

At 1 a.m., one of his closest friends brought a group of people over to Nathan and said, "Hey, dude. These people are all asking questions about if it is possible to really know God. I told them that you were a God lover and that you would answer all of our questions!"

Nathan told me that for the next hour, this group of students, who were from all over the world, asked him one question after another in all sincerity. He told them the story of Jesus, explained redemption, and told them of God's great love.

"Mom, I believe there will be people in heaven because of that final night when I got to speak all about God. It was the product and blessing of a year of loving them, praying for them, and seeking to reach out to them. Mama, it really matters to make a choice to reach out and live by faith!"

As a consequence to this choice, he wrote a book called *Wisdom Chasers* about the need for people to understand that serving God requires a choice of their will—that we must chase after God or we will be following the world's ways.

What choice will you make about becoming a lover? After all, love is a choice of our wills to give up our rights so that we may serve others. I have also come to realize that we love God by loving others.

Nathan's ideas really challenged me in my own walk with God. And when it comes to living by the ways of love, we must make a choice. Loving others is not natural; it is supernatural! Becoming a great lover does not happen by accident. We can only leave a legacy of love if we decide to make it our goal and yield our egos and will to the Holy Spirit by practicing love as an act of our worship.

This brings to mind, again, these verses that I have had to review over and over again in my life. Being strong in love does not happen all at once. It requires baby steps of practice and then doing it again and again. That is why I have needed a reminder of these verses:

"Teacher, which is the great commandment in the Law?"
And He said to him, "'You shall love the LORD your GOD
with all your heart, and with all your soul, and with all your

mind.' This is the great and foremost commandment. The
second is like it, 'You shall love your neighbor as yourself.'
On these two commandments depend the whole Law and
the Prophets."
MATTHEW 22:36-40

Jesus pretty much says love trumps all other laws. He is not looking for how much money we give. He is looking for how generously we give because of our love. He is not measuring how many laws we keep. He is watching to see if we seek to be holy and obedient because we love Him so much.

Even as I am most blessed when my children seek what is right because they love my husband and me and want to follow what we have taught them, so God wants our obedience and actions to flow out of our love for Him. He then wants us to extend that love to others.

Jesus is the model of love. He told us where love begins—by laying down our lives. That means giving up our desire to get our own way.

It means putting aside our feelings and acting in love out of obedience.

It also requires taking the initiative to say loving words, to do loving acts, and to extend unconditional love and acceptance when we are tempted to anger or self-pity.

Love will make a difference in our friendships. Any relationship, over time, will experience stress because it involves two sinful, limited people—me and whoever is my friend! So every relationship will be tested. Am I going to demand that my friend be perfect, even if I cannot be perfect? Or am I going to acknowledge my need for God to love through me, even when there is tension? If God forgives me, so I should forgive and give grace to my friendships. This is what makes us different from the world. If we serve and encourage and invest in people, they will grow because of our life-giving love.

First John says it this way: "Whoever claims to love God yet hates a brother or sister is a liar. For whoever does not love their brother and sister, whom they have seen, cannot love God, whom they have not seen" (4:20, NIV).

Love is a muscle that grows with use. The more we practice humbling ourselves and giving love out of obedience to God, the more loving we shall be. The amazing result in my own life has been that the more I humble myself to love others no matter what, the more my love and worship of God have grown because I realize how much it cost Him to be humble and give to a totally rebellious and ungrateful world. Practicing love increases your love for God.

Motherhood is a place where servant love is seen and felt. Love is the foundation of influence in the lives of your children. If you want them to love the God that you believe in, then they will learn about His generous servant love by watching your life and learning what God's love is by receiving it from you.

The very first attributes that Paul uses to describe love are found in 1 Corinthians 13:4. "Love is patient, love is kind."

Being patient with others, especially our children or family, is such a challenge. They are so dependent on us and need our time, our attention, our labor, our prayers, our training, and our patience—because it takes them a long time to grow to be mature. I believe that God gives us children as a training ground for us to truly learn what sacrificial love is like.

To others, time is equal to love. If we do not give them our time—to listen to them, to be their friend, to teach them Scripture, to care for their needs in a creative and practical way—then they will not believe it when we tell them that we love them and that God loves them. We must invest our lives in our children even as Jesus left the throne of heaven to give all of His time to His own disciples, which is who our children are to us. If Jesus gave His life and lived with them, fed them, instructed them, and loved them—can we expect to do anything less?

Then there is marriage. All marriages eventually have stress, some more than others. Yet marriage is a place where we portray the picture of God's relationship to the world. Even as Jesus calls Himself the Bridegroom and gave Himself up for His bride (the believers—His church), so marriage pictures the eternal loyalty of God to us. God will never divorce us. Hosea is a book that portrays how loyal God's love is to us. Hosea was commanded to stay loyal in his love to an adulterous woman as a picture of God's loyal love to us.

Cultivating love in marriage means learning to show respect to our spouse out of our love for God. Learning to give words of life instead of complaining. Learning to overlook the faults of our spouse because God overlooks our sin.

Peter is such an example of this. He experienced the grace and mercy of God when he denied Jesus at His time of death. Jesus prayed for Peter and still validated him as the rock, the leader, the one who would lead the disciples. And so Peter writes, out of his own experience, "Above all, love each other deeply, because love covers over a multitude of sins" (1 Peter 4:8, NIV).

He says that love covers not just one sin, but a whole mass of sin. In other words, when we love our spouses, or our children, or our friends, we should cover a multitude of their sins—over and over and over—even as we hope they will do for us.

All of my older children have told me, "Mama, we have watched you and Daddy make the choice to love each other over and over again, even when we knew it was hard. That is where we learned what it looked like to love in a mature way."

How you live your life today in choosing to love others will determine the way your children, non-Christians, your family, and your friends will learn what God's love is like. To leave a legacy of love is to leave a fragrance of His love wherever you go.

But the choice to be a good lover must start in your heart and will. Are you willing to live in the reality of God's love for you to learn what unconditional love is like? Will you determine to believe in His love for you every day?

Then will you determine that you will love your neighbor as yourself, out of your love for God? Will you practice giving yourself to others without expectation of getting anything back in return? Will you choose to forgive those who have wronged you because He forgives your sin? Do you accept your responsibility to be the lover in all relationships because others will truly know Jesus through the way the Holy Spirit lives out generous, abundant, kind love through you?

Love is the foundation for redeeming the world back to our precious Father. But God chose normal human beings to be the ones who would make His love known. He loved us, and we are blessed and redeemed by that healing, comforting, always present love. And then, out of gratitude, we choose to be that kind of love to the world in which we are living.

Reflection Questions

1. *"Love is patient." Are there people in your life who need to see your patience so that they will have time to grow? What is the most difficult part of loving others that requires patience?*

2. *"Love is kind." Kindness is an action that requires your works of service and thoughtfulness. What kindness speaks most to you in your life? What do you need to do to give kindness to others?*

3. *For most people, love equals time. In what ways are you too busy and distracted? How can you tame your schedule so that you will be more available to give time and attention to others?*

4. *"If you love me, keep my commands" (John 14:15, NIV). Have you made a choice to obey Jesus, out of your love for Him, to give your life to loving and serving others?*

5. *Make a list of people who are close to you (family, children, friends, neighbors) and whom you need to take action to love. Write down a plan of how you are going to make the time to love them better this year (e.g., write a note or an e-mail, make them a meal, visit them, or call them).*

Prayer:

Dear Heavenly Father, in a world that is lost and so far from You, help us to make the choices as You did; to love, serve, and lay down our lives so that the world may truly see Your love through us. Help us not to be just hearers of the Word, but doers. Let our love for You be reflected in the way we make choices to love others, out of gratefulness for Your constant and generous love and devotion. We love You so very much, and we want to keep our first love for You till we see You face-to-face!

Week 8: Monday

Read: Matthew 22:36-40

SOAP: Matthew 22:37-38

S Write out the **Scripture** passage for the day.

O Write down one or two **observations** from the passage.

A Write down one or two **applications** from the passage.

P **Pray** over what you learned from today's passage.

Week 8: Tuesday

Read: 1 Corinthians 13:1–3

SOAP: 1 Corinthians 13:1–3

S   Write out the **Scripture** passage for the day.

O   Write down one or two **observations** from the passage.

A   Write down one or two **applications** from the passage.

P   **Pray** over what you learned from today's passage.

Week 8: Wednesday

Read: 1 Corinthians 13:4–7

SOAP: 1 Corinthians 13:4–7

S Write out the **Scripture** passage for the day.

O Write down one or two **observations** from the passage.

A Write down one or two **applications** from the passage.

P **Pray** over what you learned from today's passage.

Week 8: Thursday

Read: 1 Corinthians 13:8-13

SOAP: 1 Corinthians 13:8, 13

S   Write out the **Scripture** passage for the day.

O   Write down one or two **observations** from the passage.

A   Write down one or two **applications** from the passage.

P   **Pray** over what you learned from today's passage.

Week 8: Friday

Read: Leviticus 19:18

SOAP: Leviticus 19:18

S Write out the **Scripture** passage for the day.

O Write down one or two **observations** from the passage.

A Write down one or two **applications** from the passage.

P **Pray** over what you learned from today's passage.

My Reflection:

Take time to write out what God has spoken to your heart during this study. How is your life going to change now that you better understand God's love for you? How can you use the stories God has given you, through your life, to give God glory and help others see how much they are loved?

About the Authors

SALLY CLARKSON cofounded and has served as the women's ministry director of Whole Heart Ministries with her husband, Clay, since 1994. As a conference speaker, the author of ten popular books, and a ministry leader, she has helped countless Christian parents build life-giving homes and raise wholehearted children for Christ. As a mother of four, she has inspired thousands of mothers since 1998 through annual Mom Heart Conferences and Mom Heart small groups. Sally encourages many through her blog posts at SallyClarkson.com and MomHeart.com, as well as through her e-books and live webinars. She began her ministry in Communist Eastern Europe with the international ministry CRU and has a passion for discipleship training.

ANGELA PERRITT is a writer, a speaker, and the founder of LoveGodGreatly.com, a nonprofit online Bible study ministry that reaches thousands of women in over seventy countries with God's Word through original Bible study materials and online community groups. She is passionate about God's Word and about inspiring, encouraging, and equipping others to love God greatly with their lives, one day at a time. Angela holds a master's degree in instructional technology from Bowling Green State University and lives with her husband and three daughters in Dallas.

$\mathcal{F}$or twenty years . . . in cities across North America . . . Women of Faith has been connecting with millions of women to share this message: "God loves you and is crazy about you!"

Long before reality TV, Women of Faith speakers were candidly sharing their real problems and challenges in life. Their courageous stories welcomed women into a circle of friends, showed them they were not alone, and offered reassurance that wherever they are in life, Jesus is right there with them.

Women of Faith points women to the truths in the Bible that bring comfort, redemption, forgiveness, confidence, challenge, reassurance, and hope.

For more information about Women of Faith events, inspiration, and encouragement, visit WomenofFaith.com.